Create protective, empowering, and healing
Energy Circles for yourself and others!

ENERGY CIRCLES

Encircle and fill your life with love,
peace, joy, health, abundance, and power!

GEORGIOS MYLONAS
GEOM!*

Important Note

The recommendations made in this book should not be considered a replacement for formal medical or mental treatment. A physician should be consulted in all matters relating to health, including any symptoms that require medical attention. Anyone who has emotional, mental, or physical problems should seek professional consultation before attempting any of these practices. While the information and the suggestions in this book are believed to be safe and accurate, the author cannot accept liability for any harm as a result of the use or misuse of these practices. This book is intended as general information and for educational purposes.

First English edition 2018

© Georgios Mylonas

All rights reserved.

No part of this publication may be reproduced or transmitted in any form or by any means, electronic or mechanical, including photocopying, recording, or by any information storage and retrieval system, without the written permission of the publisher.

Copyright © 2018 by Georgios Mylonas

Georgios Mylonas (Geom!*)

Teacher and author on methods of energy healing,
personal development and spiritual advancement

The School of Reiki, Athens
www.energiesoflight.com
www.universityofreiki.com
www.reiki.gr
e-mail: reiki@reiki.gr

Translated by Christiana Kanaki
www.christianakanaki.com

ISBN: 9781730713507

Ten percent of the proceeds from this book go to charity.

Also by Georgios Mylonas (Geom!*)

Healing, Spiritual, and Esoteric Meditations
Angelic Invocations
Angelic Symbols
Angelic Mysticism & Meditations
The Golden Codes of Shamballa
How to Cleanse the Energy of Your Space
Higher Abundance
Higher Love
Higher Healing

CONTENTS

INTRODUCING THE ENERGY CIRCLES! 9
INFINITE POSSIBILITIES 11
GIVING AND RECEIVING ENERGY 14
THE TECHNIQUE 17
PROTECTION 20
QUESTIONS AND ANSWERS 30

– Who can apply this energy technique? 30
– In which aspects and areas of life can I apply this
   technique? What energies and qualities can
   I manifest and experience? 30
– How does this technique help? 31
– What is the foundation and what are the mechanics
   behind this technique? How does it work? 31
– How can the simple design of a circle bring protection,
   love, joy, peace, or abundance into my life? Is this just a
   feel-good technique? Or is it autosuggestion? 32
– How often should I design the circles? For example,
   if I want abundance or protection, how often should
   I make the circles in order to see some results? 33
– Can anything go wrong with this technique,
   can I do harm instead of good? 33
– Can I help with health issues or cure myself
   or someone else with this method? 34

- After drawing the circles, is it necessary
  to do the visualization as well?... 34
- Besides the circle, can I make other shapes? Triangle,
  rhombus, square, or star? 34
- Should I make circles with specific colors?
  For abundance, health, protection, and so on,
  should I use specific colors? 35
- I don't have colored markers. Can I make the
  circles with a blue or black pen or using a pencil? 38
- After the technique is over, what do I do with
  the paper or papers with the circles/drawings? 38
- Can I make the circles without drawing them with
  pens/markers, but in a symbolic way, simply
  by moving my finger circularly? 39
- Can I give reiki to the circles? Can I put some
  crystal on top of the drawing? 39
- Can I make the Energy Circles for someone else?
  Should he/she know it? Should I have his/her
  permission? And how will I do the technique? 40
- Can I make Energy Circles for my family?
  Should they know it? 43
- Can I make multiple circles of different energies, for
  example, a circle of protection, a circle of abundance,
  a health circle, and so on, around my name or someone
  else's name? In other words, is it possible on the same
  paper/drawing, to have many circles, one inside
  the other, each for a different quality? 43
- Can I put many people together inside a circle? 44

– Can I make someone fall in love with me, form a relationship with me, maintain the relationship, or return back to me? Can I do it for another person in order to help him/her bring someone closer? 45

– Instead of my name, can I place in the center of the circle my space, my home, or my workplace, and make circles of protection or purification or abundance around it? 45

– How can I send positive energy to a situation? How can I help energetically an issue that concerns me? How can I heal it or find a solution to it? 46

– Can I make circles with energies that are not mentioned in this book? 46

THE ENERGIES

LOVE 51
LIGHT/POSITIVE ENERGY 61
HEALTH, HEALING THE BODY 71
PEACE AND TRANQUILITY 81
JOY AND BLISS 91
ABUNDANCE AND PROSPERITY 101
A LOVING ROMANTIC RELATIONSHIP 111
A GOOD, POSITIVE, AND HEALTHY RELATIONSHIP (HEALING OR IMPROVING A RELATIONSHIP) 121
BEAUTY 132
YOUTHFULNESS 142
IDEAL BODY WEIGHT 152

ENERGETIC CLEARING AND PURIFICATION 162
DETOXIFICATION, RELEASE OF UNHEALTHY
HABITS AND ADDICTIONS 172
RELEASE OF FEAR (OR BITTERNESS,
ANGER, GUILT, SADNESS, OR WORRY) 184
EMOTIONAL HEALING... 194
GUIDANCE, ANSWERS, CHOICES 204
WISDOM, ILLUMINATION, ENLIGHTENMENT 214

The Highest Energy

More Energy

Energy

You

INTRODUCING THE ENERGY CIRCLES!

The Energy Circles method is a simple and effective technique for focusing energy, and is a whole and complete-in-itself method of spiritual activation. By putting it into action, it will give you the potential to offer pure, positive, and vital energy and superior qualities to yourself and others; positive and beneficial energies and qualities to yourself, your family, your beloved ones, and all people! Use the Energy Circles method to manifest greater protection and power, bring forth more serenity and joy, create new abundance and prosperity, attune to higher love and harmony, receive deeper wisdom and guidance, and experience increased health and vitality.

It's probably one of the simplest methods you can use – as simple, easy, and practical as drawing a line or a circle on paper! Despite its simplicity and ease, it contains amazing power; it's an impressively powerful and effective tool of energy focusing! It is the quintessence of what is being taught in energy healing and spiritual healing workshops and it is given in this simple, practical and easy-to-use form so as to help more people. To help more – more people in number – and to help more – to a greater extent.

This system is given as a meditative energetic technique that anyone can use directly, with miraculous results. It is something I've been practicing over the years and through which

I've seen minor and major miracles taking place. It's not a strange thing, although it can always take you by surprise, just like the first time you use it! It is the natural extension and implementation of all internal laws. I have shared it with and taught it to friends and students in energy healing seminars and meditation groups, with impressive benefits for everyone involved. And everyone keeps wondering how something so small and simple can give so much power and energy! Now, this technique will be made clear and will be given clearly – it will be given to everyone!

Perhaps you've done something similar, either consciously or subconsciously! It's time to fully realize it! In the form presented here, it will directly help you to externalize your entire spiritual knowledge and all of your inner power, to put them into work, into action. To manifest your spirituality, to express your shining and most wise spirit!

Life moves in circles and so does Spirit. So, let's consciously enter these circles. And let's start new ones. New circles! Greater, higher, brighter circles!

INFINITE POSSIBILITIES

Have you ever found yourself making patterns on paper while, for example, you are talking on the phone? Or as you daydream or think about various things? Doodling scribbles, lines, shapes, drawings, sketches on paper? Well, now this will become more important! We will make it matter, and as a matter of fact, it will matter a great deal!

Imagine if you could design all good things, joy, and fulfillment, both for yourself and others. If you could place protection, give strength, and promote health. Offer love and abundance. Imagine being able to give and offer something essential and substantial, something real and true, just by designing, by making simple drawings, or sketches on paper.

Does that seem odd to you? Yet, it is possible! Think about it. A great teacher, a being of very high consciousness, a being of great wisdom and power – such a master would have the ability to bless you and give you spiritual energy. Everything would change, with just one movement of his, one word, one look. Through his thought, or intent, through his wish, with one single commandment. A great teacher would create a circle of protection around you and you would feel it! He would draw a circle of power around you and you would feel its celestial effect! A word, a wish, an intention is enough to bring more blessing, health, love, joy, peace, and abundance in your life! A teacher, an intention, an energy, a circle... you!

It is that easy for a great teacher, that easy for a being connected to the Source and the Whole, having access to unlimited love, wisdom, and power. Such a being has the ability to express all this power, wisdom, and love in so many ways. So simple and easy, so natural! And in all possible ways. With a sentence or word, with a wish or command, with a thought or intent, with a vision or prayer, with a movement or drawing. That much power, that much love, and that much wisdom!

And what does this great teacher have in common with us? So you might ask! But we, too, are moving; we follow this road. The way of the great teacher, the way of the teachers. There is a supreme and highest master in us and this master wants to be discovered and become acquainted with us! He/She wants us to follow him/her, to follow this master teacher to the very end, until we become one.

So let's get started and let's move on. Steadily, with love. With joy and gratitude, we walk the path of the great teacher inside us, we walk the way of all the great masters!

The system, the technique you hold in your hands, is a gift, a true gift from heaven and the great masters, and from your own great teacher. It's a tool, perhaps one of the most useful ones you've ever held. It will help you move in the best possible way and offer yourself and your loved ones every good, and all good. It will help you become a source and power of light, life, and positivity on earth, to become your authentic, true self; a being of greater love, wisdom, and power... a being of infinite love, wisdom, and power!

So let's start: How would it be if you had a positive circle, a circle of positivity, around yourself or around your life? Can you imagine it? Its energy? How would that be?

Imagine if a higher being, a great teacher, or even an angel made a circle of protection around you. A circle that protects you, removing all negativity, purifying you from everything with a lower vibration. A lucky circle, a powerful circle, a bright circle. A circle of abundance and prosperity. A circle of peace or a circle of joy! A circle of serenity: a circle of perfect serenity, for supreme peace! And a circle of joy: a circle made of wonderful joy to constantly emit and transmit pure joy!

Are we going to place the foundations, putting these circles within and around ourselves and our loved ones?

GIVING AND RECEIVING ENERGY

If you needed some positivity, some positive energy, how could you give it to yourself? Some positivity and strength? How could you do it energetically, internally? If you wanted to bring health, love, wisdom, protection, purity to yourself. If you wanted abundance and guidance. How would you bring these qualities to yourself? How would you direct yourself towards them? How would you align with them?

As you may already know, there are many ways, many methods, and techniques, both energetic and spiritual. First of all, you can meditate on what you want. You can imagine or visualize light showering you, surrounding you, and filling you up. Filling your entire body with this pure bright light. This light purifies, renews, and raises your vibration, your energy, it fills you with life and positivity, and it empowers you and exalts you! To visualize light around you and inside you is the single best thing you can do energetically! Then, you can focus on positive qualities: health, serenity, bliss, completeness, fulfillment, joy, love, abundance, etc. Bring the quality that you desire into your mind and then ask to receive it, asking it from your spirit, from your inner wisdom, from the higher self. From the universe or the Divine Source. You ask for it with your heart, with gratitude and love, and you remain in this state of calmness and tranquility, you become open to receive.

You can also visualize yourself being in ideal situations, you can see and feel yourself already in the desired situation: health, peace, love, abundance. Imagine what you want, as if it is already a reality. Feel it 100% and give out immense joy, appreciation, and gratitude! This is a perfect meditation so that you can experience superior qualities, bringing yourself towards them or bringing them into your life!

Beyond meditation and visualization, it is possible to use the power of speech. Write positive statements or affirmations and repeat them, mentally or out loud, several times, faithfully and powerfully. Over and over again, daily, until they are written down into your subconscious, until they become part of your energy and reality.

So, you can experience all good things, all positive energies and qualities, through meditation and visualization, but also through thinking, through speech, written and spoken, as well as through prayer, invocations, and through various other practices of energetic or spiritual nature, such as yoga, breathing exercises, and the repetition of mantras.

Energy healing methods, such as reiki and crystal therapy, also offer positive/vital energy and attune us with desirable qualities, while they teach us techniques for manifesting positive outcomes. The theory of the law of attraction, and various spiritual traditions from all around the world, and esotericism all offer a multitude of techniques to attract, manifest, and create more power, protection, purity, love, peace, abundance, freedom, bliss, and enlightenment.

Apart from the above, there is also something else... This, here, now! A complete method of focusing yourself positively and giving new breath and strength to your life. This technique is the Energy Circles. But what exactly is it and how can we practice it?

THE TECHNIQUE

In the Energy Circle technique, we design one or more circles that symbolize some energy, some quality, or a desirable state. We can design circles that symbolize protection, purification, abundance, peace, joy, love, health, power, wisdom, and guidance. Or any other energy and quality that we want to manifest in our lives!

We can do it for ourselves as well as for others, for our loved ones, but also for those who need support and empowerment. At the center of the circle, we write where this energy goes to, for whom the circle is designed. So, we write down our name or the name of someone else and then we draw the circle or circles around it.

As we do it, we have the specific intention that we chose in mind. What it symbolizes, what the circle means. For example, "Protection." We write our name and design a circle around it, keeping in mind the energy, the quality of protection. We reinforce the process with statements, confirming what we want to manifest, create, bring. For example, we design the circle around our name and say, either mentally or aloud, "I create protection," or "More protection," or something similar. Below you will find many such ideas on what to state, as the case may be.

We also use colors. We can use whatever color we want, just one color or more, and make circles with the color most closely related to the quality that we have in mind. Red brings protection and purification, while blue leads to peace and freedom. Green promotes health and harmony, and yellow radiates wisdom and power. Purple and violet are spiritual colors and give guidance and insight, while pink is the color of love. Silver is a grounding and manifesting color, while gold is the color of the highest consciousness, spirit, and Source.

We do the whole process meditatively – that is, calmly and slowly, with intent, focused and observing. We relax and take some deep breaths before, during, and after the drawing process. At the end, while we remain relaxed, we observe the energy and we stay in this energy that has been created. We can add the power of visualization, seeing in our imagination the circle or the sphere of energy that we want around us, surrounding us and filling us with its bright and positive effect!

It is an exercise of consciousness, a game, an energy game. But consciousness can do everything; it is the alpha and the omega. And energy has infinite power and there is infinite energy, infinite energy of infinite power! Infinite power and love and wisdom! Life energy, vital energy. Energy of spirit, spiritual energy. Energy of the light, light energy. You can experiment as much as you want in this exercise, in this game. It's so simple but so powerful. You have to do it to believe it and, when you believe it, do it more, over and over again! There is an inexhaustible positivity that you can absorb and an inexhaustible positivity to which you are moving.

What follows is an example of how to create more protection in our lives. Then there are answers to possible questions about the technique, about this work. Later on, the technique will be applied for more desirable energies and qualities, such as love, health, abundance, peace, and others.

Let's get things from the start! Let the circles begin... Protection!

PROTECTION

Take some sheets of white paper and a red marker.

Sit comfortably and relax.

Take a few deep breaths, at a calm and slow pace. Inhale from the nose, slowly and deeply, taking your breath deep down into your belly and lower abdomen. Breathe out from the mouth, blowing the air gently, steadily, and slowly. Do these full, conscious, energetic breaths. They will release any tension, pressure, and burden and will fill you with energy, liveliness, and positivity.

Then, simply relax, and calm down your mind and body totally. Let go, let go completely.

Feel joy and have a wonderful sense of joyful anticipation, thinking about what you are going to do! You are going to give protection to yourself, you are going to place your personal energy within greater protection – spiritual and energetic protection! You are about to bring forth and experience perfect protection, total protection, protection on all levels!

Take the marker and one sheet of paper and write your name in the center of the paper. Your forename and then your sur-

name under it. You can write your official, complete name or the one you use in your daily encounters. You can also use your middle name, if you have one. Simply write it under your forename and above your surname.

You can also just write the initials of your forename and surname. You can even not write down your name at all. Instead, you may write or draw something on the paper that represents/symbolizes you. For instance, you can make a dot, draw a star, or a human stick figure, as a symbol for yourself. What you have in mind – your intention – is the primary and most important element in this work and the design is secondary; it is merely symbolic.

Think that, while using the marker and drawing a circle around your name, this circle symbolizes the energy and the quality you want to bring forth and experience. The ideal state/condition you want to experience. In this case, it is Protection.

Draw the circle around your complete name. Do it slowly, meditatively. It does not matter how large the circle is – as long as it encircles your name, that is, until it includes you. It does not have to be a perfect circle; it can be clumsy. Also, it does not matter whether you draw the circle in a left or right direction.

Do it slowly and think that what you do has great power, great power in energetic and spiritual terms.

Keep your intention in mind while you draw the circle. What does it mean? Why are you doing this?
Affirm it, either mentally or out loud:
"I create a circle of protection around me...
A circle of protection, around me...
I place myself within a circle of protection...
Myself, within protection...
I am within protection..."

You can also repeat the quality/energy:

"Protection... Protection... Protection..."

Or you can repeat both affirmations:

"Protection... Protection... Protection...
I create a circle of protection around me...
A circle of protection around me...
I place myself within a circle of protection...
Myself, within protection...
I am within protection..."

There is no right or wrong in doing this. Do it in your own way, using your own creativity, inner guidance, and intuition. You may use your own wording, affirm it in your own way. Just have a clear intention: in this case, Protection.

Repeat and draw the circle over and over with this color, repeating the thoughts, making adjustments, and enhancing them, making the color of the circle more intense, vivid, and uniform. Each time, re-affirm your intention for protection.

Then, pause for a while and look at the circle and think once more what it stands for, what it means. Do you feel the energy? Relax and notice. You can also take some slow, full, deep breaths.

You can enhance and empower this energy even more!

Using the same red color, design a second larger circle around the first one. Think of what this second larger circle means:

"Greater protection around me...
Myself, within greater protection...
I am in greater protection...
More protection...
Even more protection...
Much more protection...
Around myself and me in the center of it..."

Keep moving the marker around, making the circle bolder and stronger. Do it in a steady, slow, and meditative manner. Keep the above statement in your mind or repeat it out loud. Once more, you can use your own words but focus on your intention for even greater protection.

Make another pause and observe the drawing, and notice how you feel its energy. It works, it starts to manifest! It is manifesting its effects and it is powerful! You can also take some more deep, slow, full breaths.

Now let's take this to the maximum, to its greatest height and power.

Make a third, even larger circle, around the second one. Again, in the color red. It symbolizes the highest possible level of energy, the greatest possible protection! Absolute, perfect, total, divine protection! Protection on all levels!

Think about this meaning, as you draw the circle, slowly and meditatively. Repeat the circle a few times, over and over, and each time, think or say out loud the following:

"Perfect protection around me...
Myself, in perfect protection...
I am within perfect protection...
The highest level of protection!
The greatest, the supreme protection!
Absolute and perfect protection!
Total and complete protection!
Protection on all levels!"

As always, you can use your own wording, keeping in mind your intention for the highest level of this energy, the greatest possible protection.

Stop and relax once more, noticing and observing everything. Feel the amazing energy and power! Stay for a few moments in this high positive state, receiving and experiencing all that goodness! You can also take some more deep, slow, full breaths.

For this third circle, the third level of this work, you can also use a different color, a golden one. The color gold symbolizes the golden light, the highest spiritual light. The highest level of energy and the highest level of consciousness; super-consciousness, spiritual or divine consciousness. The golden light is the light of Spirit, the Logos, and the Source/the Absolute. It is pure wisdom, pure love, and pure power... infinite wisdom – infinite love – infinite power and perfect wisdom – perfect love – perfect power!

This technique can be done using other colors too. Instead of the red color, you may use any color you want. You could also make more circles, as many as you want. You control and define what it is that you do, what energy/quality you create, and in what way. Just be aware, know what it is that you're doing, why you are doing each move, the purpose behind each thing.

For example, you can use all the colors, symbolizing different aspects and qualities of protection, or meaning protection on different levels and for different areas of your life.

Try both: protection with a variety of different colors and protection using only the red color, or with a combination of red and gold at the end.

You can do just one circle. Leave the drawing as it is and then, after some time has passed or even days later, add a second circle or a third one. Once again, there is no right or wrong; you will be guided. Maybe you make many circles, then decide they are not needed, and so you do the process again, with just one circle this time. Follow your intuition.

Make the process esoterically, calmly, meditatively, and make pauses to feel the energy. Take deep breaths at the beginning and at the end of this exercise and during its practice. Focus on your purpose, clarify your intention, before you begin to design and as you design. Hold your intention. Every now and then, think of why you do what you do, what it means, what it stands for. And at the end, remain in this state, meditating for a few minutes, feeling the wonderful energy, the higher level you have entered!

STRENGTHENING THE PROCESS

There are two ways to reinforce this technique: to fill the circle with color and to add visualization.

COLOR FILLING

Fill the circle with the color red. Color inside the circle line, slowly and calmly, filling in the white area, and covering your name. You do this so as to fill the space with energy. Your aura and your body. It's like filling your body with color, with energy, with the quality you want – in this case, Protection!

Think about what you are doing. Have a clear intention in your mind as you fill the circle with color:

"I fill myself with protection, with the energy of protection.
My aura, my energy, my body, is filled with protection, with the energy of protection!
Protection everywhere around me and everywhere inside me...
Protection everywhere around me and everywhere inside me...

Protection everywhere around me and everywhere inside me..."

Or you can use your own words.

Color and fill the whole circle.

You can also fill the space between the first and second circle and between the second and third circle as well, although this is not so important. Do it though, if you feel like it.

Since you have covered your name with color and you can no longer see it, rewrite it down below, below the circles, at the bottom of the paper.

VISUALIZATION

If you want to see more immediate results, add visualization into the process. You can do it at the beginning or at the end. Or twice, both at the beginning and at the end. This empowers the process to the highest degree!

Gently close your eyes, take some slow and deep breaths, and then let go. Relax your body and mind.

Visualize the circle of protection around you. You can envision a red, white, or golden circle. Or of some other color. You can also visualize a sphere – this is even better! A red protective sphere around you. Or a golden sphere of protection around you. The golden sphere is the highest energy – it is all-inclusive! It is the most intelligent and wise and the strongest and most powerful energy. It is like the sun.

Feel that the sphere is full of energy, light, and power. Full of protection. And you are inside it! You can see or feel this energy as red energy or as white or golden. In all cases, white or golden energy is ideal. White is the energy of life and it includes everything, all possibilities, while golden is the energy of Spirit and consciousness, of the Supreme Source and it symbolizes the infinite and perfect wisdom, love, and power of the absolute.

You are in the sphere of protection, within the energy of protection!

Mentally, state (or use your own words):

"I am in the sphere of protection, within the energy of protection.
The energy of protection surrounds me; it is all around me.
And the energy of protection is inside me, it is everywhere inside me.
Supreme protection!
Perfect protection!
Absolute protection!
Protection on all levels!"

You do not have to make a second or third circle or a second or third sphere. For the visualization, one circle or one sphere is enough. If, nonetheless, you feel guided to visualize more circles or spheres, go on and do it.

Finally, give thanks from your heart with the utmost love, joy, and gratitude! Open your eyes.

The highest, the most perfect protection, with infinite love and unlimited joy!

QUESTIONS AND ANSWERS

– Who can apply this energy technique?

All! Everyone, without exception, can make Energy Circles and receive the benefit of the amazing positive energy that they – so abundantly – create! You do not need any prior knowledge or skill.

– In which aspects and areas of life can I apply this technique? What energies and qualities can I manifest and experience?

In all aspects and areas and all energies and qualities! Using the Energy Circles, you can creatively focus on any positive energy and quality that you want to see in your life, as well as work energetically on every subject that concerns you. There is no limitation, as long as it is all within the Higher Good, the energy of love and of the good. Work with clear and pure intentions, love intentions, for the sake of love and for the sake of the good and only. The Higher Good, the highest possible good. Work with love and dedicate your work to love and to the good, the supreme good of all creatures.

Through this technique, you can ask for and receive a great deal, among the following: guidance and wisdom, protection and purification, strength and health, joy and fulfillment, bliss and freedom, knowledge and creativity, love and romance, beauty and youthfulness, healthy body weight and detoxification from unhealthy habits, self-awareness and illumination, achievement of goals and completion of work, overcoming difficulties and problem solving. And much more!

In this book you will find 18 themes that cover a wide range of primary needs and basic wishes for all people. Use these qualities and you can add more, intuitively and according to your needs and desires.

– How does this technique help?

This technique focuses positively and powerfully your consciousness, your mind, and your energy. It activates and awakens your inner potential, your spiritual power. It is a technique that helps us manifest more of the infinite wisdom, love, and power that we have as pure divine souls, as radiant spiritual beings.

– What is the foundation and what are the mechanics behind this technique? How does it work?

The focus of consciousness and of the mind as well as the power of intent lie at the center of this work and they are responsible for doing the miracles! Behind this work there is a superior intelligence and power, that of the spirit, the spiritual source. This technique was given by spiritual masters, great guides of the spirit, so as to activate the intention and consciousness of man to the greatest extent. To help awaken and manifest all the powers that the consciousness, the spirit of the human being has. Infinite powers, supreme energies! Powers and energies that heal and illuminate everything! Powers and energies of the universe and of the Whole, powers and energies of existence and of life, powers and energies of the infinite and of the source!

– How can the simple design of a circle bring protection, love, joy, peace, or abundance into my life? Is this just a feel-good technique? Or is it autosuggestion?

It is both! It's autosuggestion. And autosuggestion is a high ability of the mind that can generate incredible energy and power – it can even heal! It's also a technique that makes you feel good – and that's also good! Being well, feeling good is the point, the purpose, the driving force of all of our work, plans, actions, and efforts in life. So it's autosuggestion and it's also a technique to feel good, and these two are absolutely positive and beneficial!

But there is still something more! Or, rather, many things more that are not obvious at first glance. It is a method that focuses the mind and the mind is the beginning of everything. It is a method that gives energy and energy moves everything and it is everything. The more energy you place upon a condition, the higher, the more positive the experience. Energy is light, it is life, it is pure positivity. On the one hand, circles are an archetype, they have energy and power on their own, due to their shape, and on the other hand, they constitute a tool, an instrument, an opportunity to do what you know deep within and that which you can do. Circles focus the infinite energy of the world, the universe, and the self. They are that important and that powerful is this technique!

– How often should I design the circles? For example, if I want abundance or protection, how often should I make the circles in order to see some results?

There is no rule. Do it as often as you want, whenever you want to, or whenever you need to. Whenever you feel or are motivated to do it. Proceed intuitively. You can do it every now and then or every day. Once a day or many times during the day. Or even just once. As long as you do it in a focused way, meaning and feeling what you're doing and seeing it work. Most people feel that it works better, and is more effective, when they do it on a regular basis, often for a period of time. As if you are on a spiritual remedy and you need to take it at certain times per day, for a certain number of days. For example, three times a day, for a few days in a row, like for seven consecutive days. Three times a day for seven days in a row. Yes, this is a very powerful program. It is highly recommended! So, try doing the technique three times a day for seven consecutive days. Once again, if you feel guided to do more or fewer days, or more or fewer times per day, it's up to you. Follow your intuition and let the energy guide you.

– Can anything go wrong with this technique, can I do harm instead of good?

The answer is categorical: No! Nothing wrong or negative can result from this work.

– Can I help with health issues or cure myself or someone else with this method?

For any health problem, each person should consult a specialist physician. This method, like any energy and spiritual technique, in no way substitutes for medical or psychological diagnosis and treatment. Through energy and spiritual methods, we do not promise any kind of treatment.

Energy Circles is an energy method, an internal method that helps to a deeper level but also in a broader context. It can support any healing process, and it can offer support energetically. It is a meditative method that aims to enhance and complement in an energetic and spiritual way. It provides empowerment and support on a deeper, higher, holistic level, on the energetic and spiritual level. Combined with medical diagnosis and treatment, it can help you or some other person to get to the desired state of health more quickly.

– After drawing the circles, is it necessary to do the visualization as well?

It is not necessary, but it is something that greatly enhances this work. If you cannot do the visualization or do not have the time, just make the drawings.

– Besides the circle, can I make other shapes? Triangle, rhombus, square, or star?

Yes, as long as you have an intention in mind, why you are doing it, what it symbolizes, and the energy you are channeling. All shapes have an empowering and healing effect on the energy level!

The triangle exalts, raises the frequency, raises the vibration, connects with the sky.

The square is grounding, manifesting, stabilizing; it is a symbol of the earth.

The rhombus is like the square but also like two triangles together, bringing a connection between heaven and earth.

The cross symbolizes the four elements of nature but also the balance. It is also a symbol of Christ, of the Christ consciousness.

The five-pointed star symbolizes the human form, the human being in perfect health, balance, and power.

The spiral brings flow, vitality; it is a symbol of energy.

The circle symbolizes spirit, perfection, the absolute, the divine. It moves constantly, without beginning and without end. It is a symbol of completeness and totality, a symbol of protection and power. It contains everything. That's why it has been given as the ideal shape for this method!

– Should I make circles with specific colors? For abun-

dance, health, protection, and so on, should I use specific colors?

You can make any circle with whatever color you want. All colors have, to a certain extent, all qualities and all qualities are expressed, at some level, by all colors.

That means:

Protection can be expressed with every color. Each color would mean another level or another kind of protection. For example, both red and blue give protection. But the other colors can also provide energy protection. Protection to a different extent, to another level, protection of another kind or of a different aspect.

Abundance is symbolized with both red and green. But all colors are colors of abundance and can offer abundance. Healing is expressed in both green and purple. Again, however, all colors can work therapeutically.

Although all energies and qualities can be expressed in all colors and all colors have multiple energies, there are some more frequent and stronger connections.

The main energies and qualities for each color:

Red: Fire, Protection, Purification, Power, Abundance, Grounding
Orange: Vitality, Joy, Work, Relationships, Romance

Yellow: Knowledge, Wisdom, Strength, Balance, Confidence, Happiness
Green: Emotions, Physical Health, Abundance
Turquoise: Childlikeness, Creativity, Playfulness, Joy
Blue: Tranquility, Peace, Freedom, Expression, Communication
Purple: Mind, Intuition, Clairvoyance, Spirituality, Spiritual Healing
Violet: Spiritual Healing, Purification, Spiritual Love, Guidance
White: Light, Energy of Life, Vitality, Purity
Pink: Love, Care
Silver: Grounding, Balance, Beauty, Youthfulness
Gold: Highest Consciousness and Supreme Energy, Soul and Spirit, Divine Source and Divine Love-Wisdom-Power.

The main colors for each energy and quality:

Protection: Red, Blue
Love: Pink, Fuchsia
Positive Energy, Light: White, Yellow
Health, Physical Healing: Green, Purple, White
Peace, Serenity: Blue, Green
Joy, Bliss: Orange, Yellow
Abundance, Prosperity: Green, Red
Romance, Love Life, Companionship: Orange, Red
Good, Positive, Enlightened Relationships: Orange, Green
Beauty, Youthfulness, Healthy Body Weight: Silver, Yellow
Cleansing, Clearing Energies and Influences: Red, Silver, Gold
Overcoming Negative Habits and Dependencies: Orange, Yellow, Red, Green

Emotional Healing: Green, Blue, Yellow
Guidance, Choices, Decisions: Purple, Violet, Gold
Wisdom, Enlightenment: Gold, Yellow, Purple, Violet

These are the colors that are suggested in the following pages, for the application of the technique for different energies and qualities. However, you can experiment freely with all colors. There are no mistakes.

– I don't have colored markers. Can I make the circles with a blue or black pen or using a pencil?

Of course. You can make the circles using a pen or pencil. And any other tool that writes, sketches or draws!

– After the technique is over, what do I do with the paper or papers with the circles/drawings?

You can save them, keep them somewhere, or burn them. Fire is the element of the spirit, so by burning the papers, you surrender all the energies to spirit, to the higher element. Always be careful when burning paper, do it in the sink, away from anything flammable.

If you decide to keep the paper, you can place a crystal on it, for example, a clear quartz, after you have cleansed and charged it energetically. Quartz strengthens the intention and gives light and positivity everywhere and always, in all issues and situations. To clean it, hold the crystal under running cold water for a while, having the intention of cleaning the crystal in your mind. Then, leave it in a bowl of coarse salt for a few hours. After you take it out of the salt, place it in direct sunlight for a few hours. Then, charge it some more inside your palms, holding the crystal with love and respect for a few minutes, keeping in mind the intention of activating and charging the crystal. It is now ready, shiny, and alive! Full of energy, love, and light! Place it on the paper, in the center of the circle/circles. The crystal will hold within its radiant aura the power of the circle!

– Can I make the circles without drawing them with pens/markers, but in a symbolic way, simply by moving my finger circularly?

Draw circles with your finger on the floor, on the mat or outside, on soil or on sand. In these cases, you simply trace your name with your finger and then you move your finger cyclically, designing the circle or circles. If you do it on sand or soil, you can engrave the circle by passing your finger cyclically on the sand or soil, pressing it slightly so as to make the circles visible.

– Can I give reiki to the circles? Can I put some crystal on top of the drawing?

Yes and yes! If you have been initiated to reiki or have been trained in any other energy healing technique, just put your hands over the circles, then focus, relax, and observe. Feel the vital energy flowing from your palms, activating and charging the drawing and its intention, empowering the quality it invokes and creates. If you work with crystals and have studied crystal healing, do not hesitate to put your knowledge into practice, by placing your crystals on the circles! Remember to cleanse and charge/activate the crystals in the way you know best before each use. Experiment abundantly, intuitively, and in perfect freedom, empowering the circles with crystals, reiki, and any other energy healing technique!

– Can I make the Energy Circles for someone else? Should he/she know it? Should I have his/her permission? And how will I do the technique?

Yes, of course, you can make circles for other people too! For someone who asks for help and support, for someone who needs healing, physical or emotional support. You can give protection, love, abundance, vitality, joy, peace, and all the good things to others in the same way you did to yourself!

But the persons have to know that you are working energetically on them, that you are giving them positive energy and positive qualities! Ask the individuals beforehand if they want to receive a positive boost, an empowerment. Do not violate their free will in any case, whether they refuse or have second thoughts and objections.

If you cannot get their approval due to circumstances, ask their higher self (their spiritual self) to accept or reject this energy. Wish and intend the Highest Good and work with love and without selfishness or attachment, without a desire to control or interfere with your personal interests and judgments. Work solely for the Highest Good of the person, whichever that may be. Only the Divine and the soul/spirit of the person know what is best for the individual and his/her evolution. You should accept this and work from the highest point of freedom, love, and respect for the Highest Good.

At the beginning and at the end of the technique, state:

"Beloved Higher Self of ...... (name of person), I send this quality for the Highest Good of ...... (name of person). I fully respect his/her free will and free choice. ...... (name of person) is free to accept or reject this energy or to receive it whenever necessary! I go beyond my ego and send this energy with complete freedom, supreme love, and absolute respect, without any trace of judgment, control, enforcement, manipulation or interference."

Write the person's name in the center of the circle/circles and have the person in your mind as you do the process, at the beginning and at the end. In the statements you make, put the person's name and speak in the third person instead of the first person.

FOR PROTECTION

Intention/statements as you draw the first circle:

"Protection... Protection... Protection...
I create a circle of protection around ...... (name of person).
Circle of protection around ...... (name of person)...

I place ...... (name of person) within protection...
...... (name of person) is now within protection...
He/She is protected."

Intention/statements for the second circle:

"Greater protection around ...... (name of person)...
...... (name of person) is within greater protection.
He/She is more protected...
More protection...
Even more protection...
Much more protection ...
All around him/her and he/she is right in the center ... "

Intention/statements for the third circle:

"Perfect protection around ...... (name of person)...
...... (name of person) is in perfect protection.
He/She is in perfect protection...
The highest level of protection!
The greatest, the supreme protection!
Absolute and perfect protection!
Total and complete protection!
Protection on all levels!"

Similarly, to create other Energy Circles, circles of Healing and Health, Abundance, Peace, Joy, Love, and all the other qualities, use the above statements and simply substitute the word Protection for the desired quality – Healing and Health, Abundance, Peace, Joy, Love, and all others.

For the visualization process, instead of yourself, visualize the person to whom you send the energy within the sphere of the desired energy/quality.

– Can I make Energy Circles for my family? Should they know it?

You can make the circles for the whole family! And it's perfect! An act of love! A wave of positivity for everyone! Just write down "my family" and make the circles around it. Since you write down "my family," it is nonspecific, so you don't need to ask for permission or notify anyone. The energy goes where it is needed and there is no risk of enforcement, manipulation, or intervention. It is clearly and purely a beautiful and positive act of love and good for all!

– Can I make multiple circles of different energies, for example, a circle of protection, a circle of abundance, a health circle, and so on, around my name or someone else's name? In other words, is it possible on the same paper/drawing, to have many circles, one inside the other, each for a different quality?

Yes, it is possible, although it is better to do the process separately for each different energy/quality. That is, write the name and make circles for protection around it, and then, at some other part of the paper or on another piece of paper, write the name again and make circles of abundance this time and then, elsewhere on the paper or on another paper, write the name again and make circles for healing and health around it and so on. It is clearer and more focused this way. If, however, you are guided to do as you suggested, to write down the name and then draw multiple circles of different energies/qualities around it in the same drawing, then go ahead and do it – there is no wrong.

– Can I put many people together inside a circle?

You can put people that have something in common together inside a circle. For example: my family, my students, my friends, my clients, my colleagues, the patients in this hospital, the people in this place, the people who have that kind of problem, the people associated with that specific work or purpose, etc. When you put a lot of people in a circle, sending energy is mild and general, energy goes where it is needed, and the energy work is not intrusive. You do not have to ask for permission – the energy goes wherever it is needed, and you do not interfere with the free will of people with your own judgments or wishes. It is like praying for their general/Higher Good.

In general, however, it is better to make separate circles for different people. It is more structured and focused and works best energetically. The energy is deeper and more direct. If two or more people ask for energy help, do it on different sheets of paper, making different circles. If they have not asked for it and you want to help them, you should first ask for their permission in order to perform the energy work. In case you cannot ask them, invoke their higher self, as explained above.

— Can I make someone fall in love with me, form a relationship with me, maintain the relationship, or return back to me? Can I do it for another person in order to help him/her bring someone closer?

No! The answer is a strong, absolute, and clear-cut no! Do not attempt it. This is something that is not good spiritually, therefore it is not good on any level. Your freedom stops right where the other person's freedom starts. And the other person's freedom is supreme, absolute, and sacred! Any violation of another person's free will has a harsh effect and it takes you back on your evolution path. Nevertheless, you can create circles of love and romance and circles for a good romantic relationship without specifying the other person, and by allowing the superior element, the superior intelligence of All to take action and orchestrate everything, by choosing the best for you or the best for the person you want to help! Ask and you shall receive and trust, absolutely trust, that the best will come – the best and only that!

— Instead of my name, can I place in the center of the circle my space, my home, or my workplace, and make circles of protection or purification or abundance around it?

What an exquisite idea! Write down "My Home" or "My Workspace" and make circles around it for all the wonderful things you want to see manifesting! Protection! Serenity! Peace! Health! Joy! Love! Clarity! Harmony! Inspiration! Abundance! Positive Flow! All positive and good things!

– How can I send positive energy to a situation? How can I help energetically an issue that concerns me? How can I heal it or find a solution to it?

Write the subject that concerns you with a word or sentence and make Energy Circles around it. Choose the quality that you think is related to your subject or experiment with different ones. You can simply make circles of positive energy/light around it.

– Can I make circles with energies that are not mentioned in this book?

Yes, you can make circles for every single thing. Circles are a way to focus the infinite power of your consciousness and to manifest more energy and positive qualities in life – your life and the life of others.

You can do Energy Circles for whatever you can imagine and for everything you need. To mention a few:

Energy Circles for a Strong Memory

Energy Circles for a Clear Mind

Energy Circles for Conceiving a Baby

Energy Circles for a Good Pregnancy

Energy Circles for a Good Night's Sleep

Energy Circles for Deep Relaxation

Energy Circles for a New Start

Energy Circles for Pain Relief

Energy Circles for Grounding

Energy Circles for Angelic Connection

Energy Circles for Forgiveness

Energy Circles for a Good Journey

Energy Circles for Finding a Job or a New Home

Energy Circles for Success

Energy Circles for Achieving a Goal

Energy Circles for the Completion of a Project

Energy Circles for Unblocking and Healing an Issue

Energy Circles for Improving a Situation

And so many others!

THE ENERGIES

We have already seen the Energy Circle technique for Protection. Next, you will find 17 more energies and qualities that you can create, manifest, bring or grow in your life!

Have the best circles, with love and joy!

LOVE

LIGHT/POSITIVE ENERGY

HEALTH, HEALING THE BODY

PEACE AND TRANQUILITY

JOY AND BLISS

ABUNDANCE AND PROSPERITY

A LOVING ROMANTIC RELATIONSHIP

A GOOD, POSITIVE, AND HEALTHY RELATIONSHIP (HEALING OR IMPROVING A RELATIONSHIP)

BEAUTY

YOUTHFULNESS

IDEAL BODY WEIGHT

ENERGETIC CLEARING AND PURIFICATION

DETOXIFICATION, RELEASE OF UNHEALTHY HABITS AND ADDICTIONS

RELEASE OF FEAR (OR BITTERNESS, ANGER, GUILT, SADNESS, OR WORRY)

EMOTIONAL HEALING

GUIDANCE, ANSWERS, CHOICES

WISDOM, ILLUMINATION, ENLIGHTENMENT

ENERGY CIRCLES

The Highest Energy

More Energy

Energy

You

LOVE

Take some sheets of white paper and a pink marker.

Sit comfortably and relax.

Take a few deep breaths, at a calm and slow pace. Inhale from the nose, slowly and deeply, taking your breath deep down into your belly and lower abdomen. Breathe out from the mouth, blowing the air gently, steadily, and slowly. Do these full, conscious, energetic breaths. They will release any tension, pressure, and burden and will fill you with energy, liveliness, and positivity.

Then, simply relax, and calm down your mind and body totally. Let go, let go completely.

Feel joy and have a wonderful sense of joyful anticipation, thinking about what you are going to do! You are going to give love to yourself, you are going to place your personal energy within greater love – spiritual and energetic love! You are about to bring forth and experience perfect love, total love, love on all levels!

Take the marker and one sheet of paper and write your name in the center of the paper. Your forename and then your sur-

name under it. You can write your official, complete name or the one you use in your daily encounters. You can also use your middle name, if you have one. Simply write it under your forename and above your surname.

You can also just write the initials of your forename and surname. You can even not write down your name at all. Instead, you may write or draw something on the paper that represents/symbolizes you. For instance, you can make a dot, draw a star, or a human stick figure, as a symbol for yourself. What you have in mind – your intention – is the primary and most important element in this work and the design is secondary; it is merely symbolic.

Think that, while using the marker and drawing a circle around your name, this circle symbolizes the energy and the quality you want to bring forth and experience. The ideal state/condition you want to experience. In this case, it is Love.

Draw the circle around your complete name. Do it slowly, meditatively. It does not matter how large the circle is – as long as it encircles your name, that is, until it includes you. It does not have to be a perfect circle; it can be clumsy. Also, it does not matter whether you draw the circle in a left or right direction.

Do it slowly and think that what you do has great power, great power in energetic and spiritual terms.

Keep your intention in mind while you draw the circle. What does it mean? Why are you doing this?
Affirm it, either mentally or out loud:

"I create a circle of love around me...
A circle of love, around me...
I place myself within a circle of love...
Myself, within love...
I am within love..."

You can also repeat the quality/energy:

"Love... Love... Love..."

Or you can repeat both affirmations:

"Love... Love... Love...
I create a circle of love around me...
A circle of love, around me...
I place myself within a circle of love...
Myself, within love...
I am within love..."

There is no right or wrong in doing this. Do it in your own way, using your own creativity, inner guidance, and intuition. You may use your own wording, affirm it in your own way. Just have a clear intention: in this case, Love.

Repeat and draw the circle over and over with this color, repeating the thoughts, making adjustments, and enhancing

them, making the color of the circle more intense, vivid, and uniform. Each time, re-affirm your intention for love.

Then, pause for a while and look at the circle and think once more what it stands for, what it means. Do you feel the energy? Relax and notice. You can also take some slow, full, deep breaths.

You can enhance and empower this energy even more!

Using the same pink color, design a second larger circle around the first one. Think of what this second larger circle means:

"Greater love around me...
Myself, within greater love...
I am in greater love...
More love...
Even more love...
Much more love...
Around myself and me in the center of it..."

Keep moving the marker around, making the circle bolder and stronger. Do it in a steady, slow, and meditative manner. Keep the above statement in your mind or repeat it out loud. Once more, you can use your own words but focus on your intention for even greater love.

Make another pause and observe the drawing, and notice how you feel its energy. It works, it starts to manifest! It is manifesting its effects and it is powerful! You can also take some more deep, slow, full breaths.
Now let's take this to the maximum, to its greatest height and power.

Make a third, even larger circle, around the second one. Again, in the color pink. It symbolizes the highest possible level of energy, the greatest possible love! Absolute, perfect, total, divine love! Love on all levels!

Think about this meaning, as you draw the circle, slowly and meditatively. Repeat the circle a few times, over and over, and each time, think or say out loud the following:

"Perfect love around me...
Myself, in perfect love...
I am within perfect love...
The highest level of love!
The greatest, the supreme love!
Absolute and perfect love!
Total and complete love!
Love on all levels!"

As always, you can use your own wording, keeping in mind your intention for the highest level of this energy, the greatest possible love.

Stop and relax once more, noticing and observing everything.

Feel the amazing energy and power! Stay for a few moments in this high positive state, receiving and experiencing all that goodness! You can also take some more deep, slow, full breaths.

For this third circle, the third level of this work, you can also use a different color, a golden one. The color gold symbolizes the golden light, the highest spiritual light. The highest level of energy and the highest level of consciousness; super-consciousness, spiritual or divine consciousness. The golden light is the light of Spirit, the Logos, and the Source/the Absolute. It is pure wisdom, pure love, and pure power... infinite wisdom – infinite love – infinite power and perfect wisdom – perfect love – perfect power!

This technique can be done using other colors too. Instead of the pink color, you may use any color you want. You could also make more circles, as many as you want. You control and define what it is that you do, what energy/quality you create, and in what way. Just be aware, know what it is that you're doing, why you are doing each move, the purpose behind each thing.

For example, you can use all the colors, symbolizing different aspects and qualities of love, or meaning love on different levels and for different areas of your life.

Try both: love with a variety of different colors and love using only the pink color, or with a combination of pink and gold at the end.

You can do just one circle. Leave the drawing as it is and then, after some time has passed or even days later, add a second circle or a third one. Once again, there is no right or wrong; you will be guided. Maybe you make many circles, then decide they are not needed, and so you do the process again, with just one circle this time. Follow your intuition.

Make the process esoterically, calmly, meditatively, and make pauses to feel the energy. Take deep breaths at the beginning and at the end of this exercise and during its practice. Focus on your purpose, clarify your intention, before you begin to design and as you design. Hold your intention. Every now and then, think of why you do what you do, what it means, what it stands for. And at the end, remain in this state, meditating for a few minutes, feeling the wonderful energy, the higher level you have entered!

STRENGTHENING THE PROCESS

There are two ways to reinforce this technique: to fill the circle with color and to add visualization.

COLOR FILLING

Fill the circle with the color pink. Color inside the circle line, slowly and calmly, filling in the white area, and covering your name. You do this so as to fill the space with energy. Your aura and your body. It's like filling your body with color, with energy, with the quality you want – in this case, Love!

Think about what you are doing. Have a clear intention in your mind as you fill the circle with color:

"I fill myself with love, with the energy of love.
My aura, my energy, my body, is filled with love, with the energy of love!
Love everywhere around me and everywhere inside me...
Love everywhere around me and everywhere inside me...
Love everywhere around me and everywhere inside me... "

Or you can use your own words.

Color and fill the whole circle.

You can also fill the space between the first and second circle and between the second and third circle as well, although this is not so important. Do it though, if you feel like it.

Since you have covered your name with color and you can no longer see it, rewrite it down below, below the circles, at the bottom of the paper.

VISUALIZATION

If you want to see more immediate results, add visualization into the process. You can do it at the beginning or at the end. Or twice, both at the beginning and at the end. This empowers the process to the highest degree!

Gently close your eyes, take some slow and deep breaths, and then let go. Relax your body and mind.

Visualize the circle of love around you. You can envision a pink, white, or golden circle. Or of some other color. You can also visualize a sphere – this is even better! A pink loving sphere around you. Or a golden sphere of love around you. The golden sphere is the highest energy – it is all-inclusive! It is the most intelligent and wise and the strongest and most powerful energy. It is like the sun.

Feel that the sphere is full of energy, light, and power. Full of love. And you are inside it! You can see or feel this energy as pink energy or as white or golden. In all cases, white or golden energy is ideal. White is the energy of life and it includes everything, all possibilities, while golden is the energy of Spirit and consciousness, of the Supreme Source and it symbolizes the infinite and perfect wisdom, love, and power of the absolute.

You are in the sphere of love, within the energy of love!

Mentally, state (or use your own words):

"I am in the sphere of love, within the energy of love.
The energy of love surrounds me; it is all around me.
And the energy of love is inside me, it is everywhere inside me.
Supreme love!
Perfect love!
Absolute love!
Love on all levels!"

You do not have to make a second or third circle or a second or third sphere. For the visualization, one circle or one sphere is enough. If, nonetheless, you feel guided to visualize more circles or spheres, go on and do it.

Finally, give thanks from your heart with the utmost love, joy, and gratitude! Open your eyes.

The highest, the most perfect love, with infinite light and unlimited joy!

LIGHT/POSITIVE ENERGY

Take some sheets of white paper and a yellow marker.

Sit comfortably and relax.

Take a few deep breaths, at a calm and slow pace. Inhale from the nose, slowly and deeply, taking your breath deep down into your belly and lower abdomen. Breathe out from the mouth, blowing the air gently, steadily, and slowly. Do these full, conscious, energetic breaths. They will release any tension, pressure, and burden and will fill you with energy, liveliness, and positivity.

Then, simply relax, and calm down your mind and body totally. Let go, let go completely.

Feel joy and have a wonderful sense of joyful anticipation, thinking about what you are going to do! You are going to give light/positive energy to yourself, you are going to place your personal energy within greater light/positive energy – spiritual and energetic light/positive energy! You are about to bring forth and experience perfect light/positive energy, total light/positive energy, light/positive energy on all levels!

Take the marker and one sheet of paper and write your name in the center of the paper. Your forename and then your sur-

name under it. You can write your official, complete name or the one you use in your daily encounters. You can also use your middle name, if you have one. Simply write it under your forename and above your surname.

You can also just write the initials of your forename and surname. You can even not write down your name at all. Instead, you may write or draw something on the paper that represents/symbolizes you. For instance, you can make a dot, draw a star, or a human stick figure, as a symbol for yourself. What you have in mind – your intention – is the primary and most important element in this work and the design is secondary; it is merely symbolic.

Think that, while using the marker and drawing a circle around your name, this circle symbolizes the energy and the quality you want to bring forth and experience. The ideal state/condition you want to experience. In this case, it is Light/Positive Energy.

Draw the circle around your complete name. Do it slowly, meditatively. It does not matter how large the circle is – as long as it encircles your name, that is, until it includes you. It does not have to be a perfect circle; it can be clumsy. Also, it does not matter whether you draw the circle in a left or right direction.

Do it slowly and think that what you do has great power, great power in energetic and spiritual terms.

Keep your intention in mind while you draw the circle. What does it mean? Why are you doing this?
Affirm it, either mentally or out loud:

"I create a circle of light/positive energy around me...
A circle of light/positive energy, around me...
I place myself within a circle of light/positive energy...
Myself, within light/positive energy...
I am within light/positive energy..."

You can also repeat the quality/energy:

"Light/positive energy... Light/positive energy... Light/positive energy..."

Or you can repeat both affirmations:

"Light/positive energy... Light/positive energy... Light/positive energy...
I create a circle of light/positive energy around me...
A circle of light/positive energy around me...
I place myself within a circle of light/positive energy...
Myself, within light/positive energy...
I am within light/positive energy..."

There is no right or wrong in doing this. Do it in your own way, using your own creativity, inner guidance, and intuition. You may use your own wording, affirm it in your own way. Just have a clear intention: in this case, Light/Positive Energy.

Repeat and draw the circle over and over with this color, repeating the thoughts, making adjustments, and enhancing them, making the color of the circle more intense, vivid, and uniform. Each time, re-affirm your intention for light/positive energy.

Then, pause for a while and look at the circle and think once more what it stands for, what it means. Do you feel the energy? Relax and notice. You can also take some slow, full, deep breaths.

You can enhance and empower this energy even more!

Using the same yellow color, design a second larger circle around the first one. Think of what this second larger circle means:

"Greater light/positive energy around me...
Myself, within greater light/positive energy...
I am in greater light/positive energy...
More light/positive energy...
Even more light/positive energy...
Much more light/positive energy...
Around myself and me in the center of it..."

Keep moving the marker around, making the circle bolder and stronger. Do it in a steady, slow, and meditative manner. Keep the above statement in your mind or repeat it out loud. Once more, you can use your own words but focus on your intention for even greater light/positive energy.

Make another pause and observe the drawing, and notice how you feel its energy. It works, it starts to manifest! It is manifesting its effects and it is powerful! You can also take some more deep, slow, full breaths.

Now let's take this to the maximum, to its greatest height and power.

Make a third, even larger circle, around the second one. Again, in the color yellow. It symbolizes the highest possible level of energy, the greatest possible light/positive energy! Absolute, perfect, total, divine light/positive energy! Light/positive energy on all levels!

Think about this meaning, as you draw the circle, slowly and meditatively. Repeat the circle a few times, over and over, and each time, think or say out loud the following:

"Perfect light/positive energy around me…
Myself, in perfect light/positive energy…
I am within perfect light/positive energy…
The highest level of light/positive energy!
The greatest, the supreme light/positive energy!
Absolute and perfect light/positive energy!
Total and complete light/positive energy!
Light/positive energy on all levels!"

As always, you can use your own wording, keeping in mind your intention for the highest level of this energy, the greatest possible light/positive energy.

Stop and relax once more, noticing and observing everything. Feel the amazing energy and power! Stay for a few moments in this high positive state, receiving and experiencing all that goodness! You can also take some more deep, slow, full breaths.

For this third circle, the third level of this work, you can also use a different color, a golden one. The color gold symbolizes the golden light, the highest spiritual light. The highest level of energy and the highest level of consciousness; super-consciousness, spiritual or divine consciousness. The golden light is the light of Spirit, the Logos, and the Source/the Absolute. It is pure wisdom, pure love, and pure power... infinite wisdom – infinite love – infinite power and perfect wisdom – perfect love – perfect power!

This technique can be done using other colors too. Instead of the yellow color, you may use any color you want. You could also make more circles, as many as you want. You control and define what it is that you do, what energy/quality you create, and in what way. Just be aware, know what it is that you're doing, why you are doing each move, the purpose behind each thing.

For example, you can use all the colors, symbolizing different aspects and qualities of light/positive energy, or meaning light/positive energy on different levels and for different areas of your life.

Try both: light/positive energy with a variety of different

colors and light/positive energy using only the yellow color, or with a combination of yellow and gold at the end.

You can do just one circle. Leave the drawing as it is and then, after some time has passed or even days later, add a second circle or a third one. Once again, there is no right or wrong; you will be guided. Maybe you make many circles, then decide they are not needed, and so you do the process again, with just one circle this time. Follow your intuition.

Make the process esoterically, calmly, meditatively, and make pauses to feel the energy. Take deep breaths at the beginning and at the end of this exercise and during its practice. Focus on your purpose, clarify your intention, before you begin to design and as you design. Hold your intention. Every now and then, think of why you do what you do, what it means, what it stands for. And at the end, remain in this state, meditating for a few minutes, feeling the wonderful energy, the higher level you have entered!

STRENGTHENING THE PROCESS

There are two ways to reinforce this technique: to fill the circle with color and to add visualization.

COLOR FILLING

Fill the circle with the color yellow. Color inside the circle line, slowly and calmly, filling in the white area, and covering your name. You do this so as to fill the space with energy. Your aura and your body. It's like filling your body with color, with energy, with the quality you want – in this case, Light/Positive Energy!

Think about what you are doing. Have a clear intention in your mind as you fill the circle with color:

"I fill myself with light/positive energy, with the energy of light/positive energy.
My aura, my energy, my body, is filled with light/positive energy, with the energy of light/positive energy!
Light/positive energy everywhere around me and everywhere inside me...
Light/positive energy everywhere around me and everywhere inside me...
Light/positive energy everywhere around me and everywhere inside me... "

Or you can use your own words.

Color and fill the whole circle.

You can also fill the space between the first and second circle and between the second and third circle as well, although this is not so important. Do it though, if you feel like it.

Since you have covered your name with color and you can no longer see it, rewrite it down below, below the circles, at the bottom of the paper.

VISUALIZATION

If you want to see more immediate results, add visualization into the process. You can do it at the beginning or at the end. Or twice, both at the beginning and at the end. This empowers the process to the highest degree!

Gently close your eyes, take some slow and deep breaths, and then let go. Relax your body and mind.

Visualize the circle of light/positive energy around you. You can envision a yellow, white, or golden circle. Or of some other color. You can also visualize a sphere – this is even better! A yellow sphere of light and positive energy around you. Or a golden sphere of light/positive energy around you. The golden sphere is the highest energy – it is all-inclusive! It is the most intelligent and wise and the strongest and most powerful energy. It is like the sun.

Feel that the sphere is full of energy, light, and power. Full of light/positive energy. And you are inside it! You can see or feel this energy as yellow energy or as white or golden. In all cases, white or golden energy is ideal. White is the energy of life and it includes everything, all possibilities, while golden is the energy of Spirit and consciousness, of the Supreme Source and it symbolizes the infinite and perfect wisdom, love, and power of the absolute.

You are in the sphere of light/positive energy, within the energy of light/positive energy!

Mentally, state (or use your own words):

"I am in the sphere of light/positive energy, within the energy of light/positive energy.
The energy of light/positive energy surrounds me; it is all around me.
And the energy of light/positive energy is inside me, it is everywhere inside me.
Supreme light/positive energy!
Perfect light/positive energy!
Absolute light/positive energy!
Light/positive energy on all levels!"

You do not have to make a second or third circle or a second or third sphere. For the visualization, one circle or one sphere is enough. If, nonetheless, you feel guided to visualize more circles or spheres, go on and do it.

Finally, give thanks from your heart with the utmost love, joy, and gratitude! Open your eyes.

The highest, the most perfect light/positive energy, with infinite love and unlimited joy!

HEALTH, HEALING THE BODY

Take some sheets of white paper and a green marker.

Sit comfortably and relax.

Take a few deep breaths, at a calm and slow pace. Inhale from the nose, slowly and deeply, taking your breath deep down into your belly and lower abdomen. Breathe out from the mouth, blowing the air gently, steadily, and slowly. Do these full, conscious, energetic breaths. They will release any tension, pressure, and burden and will fill you with energy, liveliness, and positivity.

Then, simply relax, and calm down your mind and body totally. Let go, let go completely.

Feel joy and have a wonderful sense of joyful anticipation, thinking about what you are going to do! You are going to give healing to yourself, you are going to place your personal energy within greater health – spiritual and energetic health! You are about to bring forth and experience perfect health, total health, health on all levels!

Take the marker and one sheet of paper and write your name in the center of the paper. Your forename and then your surname under it. You can write your official, complete name or the one you use in your daily encounters. You can also use your middle name, if you have one. Simply write it under your forename and above your surname.

You can also just write the initials of your forename and surname. You can even not write down your name at all. Instead, you may write or draw something on the paper that represents/symbolizes you. For instance, you can make a dot, draw a star, or a human stick figure, as a symbol for yourself. What you have in mind – your intention – is the primary and most important element in this work and the design is secondary; it is merely symbolic.

Think that, while using the marker and drawing a circle around your name, this circle symbolizes the energy and the quality you want to bring forth and experience. The ideal state/condition you want to experience. In this case, it is Health.

Draw the circle around your complete name. Do it slowly, meditatively. It does not matter how large the circle is – as long as it encircles your name, that is, until it includes you. It does not have to be a perfect circle; it can be clumsy. Also, it does not matter whether you draw the circle in a left or right direction.

Do it slowly and think that what you do has great power, great power in energetic and spiritual terms.

Keep your intention in mind while you draw the circle. What does it mean? Why are you doing this?

Affirm it, either mentally or out loud:
"I create a circle of health around me...
A circle of health, around me...
I place myself within a circle of health...
Myself, within health...
I am within health..."

You can also repeat the quality/energy:

"Health... Health... Health..."

Or you can repeat both affirmations:

"Health... Health... Health...
I create a circle of health around me...
A circle of health around me...
I place myself within a circle of health...
Myself, within health...
I am within health..."

There is no right or wrong in doing this. Do it in your own way, using your own creativity, inner guidance, and intuition. You may use your own wording, affirm it in your own way. Just have a clear intention: in this case, Health.

Repeat and draw the circle over and over with this color, repeating the thoughts, making adjustments, and enhancing them, making the color of the circle more intense, vivid, and uniform. Each time, re-affirm your intention for health.

Then, pause for a while and look at the circle and think once more what it stands for, what it means. Do you feel the energy? Relax and notice. You can also take some slow, full, deep breaths.

You can enhance and empower this energy even more!

Using the same green color, design a second larger circle around the first one. Think of what this second larger circle means:

"Greater health around me...
Myself, within greater health...
I am in greater health...
More health...
Even more health...
Much more health...
Around myself and me in the center of it..."

Keep moving the marker around, making the circle bolder and stronger. Do it in a steady, slow, and meditative manner. Keep the above statement in your mind or repeat it out loud. Once more, you can use your own words but focus on your intention for even greater health.

Make another pause and observe the drawing, and notice how you feel its energy. It works, it starts to manifest! It is manifesting its effects and it is powerful! You can also take some more deep, slow, full breaths.

Now let's take this to the maximum, to its greatest height and power.

Make a third, even larger circle, around the second one. Again, in the color green. It symbolizes the highest possible level of energy, the greatest possible health! Absolute, perfect, total, divine health! Health on all levels!

Think about this meaning, as you draw the circle, slowly and meditatively. Repeat the circle a few times, over and over, and each time, think or say out loud the following:

"Perfect health around me...
Myself, in perfect health...
I am within perfect health...
The highest level of health!
The greatest, the supreme health!
Absolute and perfect health!
Total and complete health!
Health on all levels!"

As always, you can use your own wording, keeping in mind your intention for the highest level of this energy, the greatest possible health.

Stop and relax once more, noticing and observing everything. Feel the amazing energy and power! Stay for a few moments in this high positive state, receiving and experiencing all that goodness! You can also take some more deep, slow, full breaths.

For this third circle, the third level of this work, you can also use a different color, a golden one. The color gold symbolizes the golden light, the highest spiritual light. The highest level of energy and the highest level of consciousness; super-consciousness, spiritual or divine consciousness. The golden light is the light of Spirit, the Logos, and the Source/the Absolute. It is pure wisdom, pure love, and pure power... infinite wisdom – infinite love – infinite power and perfect wisdom – perfect love – perfect power!

This technique can be done using other colors too. Instead of the green color, you may use any color you want. You could also make more circles, as many as you want. You control and define what it is that you do, what energy/quality you create, and in what way. Just be aware, know what it is that you're doing, why you are doing each move, the purpose behind each thing.

For example, you can use all the colors, symbolizing different aspects and qualities of health, or meaning health on different levels and for different areas of your life.

Try both: health with a variety of different colors and health using only the green color, or with a combination of green and gold at the end.

You can do just one circle. Leave the drawing as it is and then, after some time has passed or even days later, add a second circle or a third one. Once again, there is no right or wrong; you will be guided. Maybe you make many circles, then decide they are not needed, and so you do the process again, with just one circle this time. Follow your intuition.

Make the process esoterically, calmly, meditatively, and make pauses to feel the energy. Take deep breaths at the beginning and at the end of this exercise and during its practice. Focus on your purpose, clarify your intention, before you begin to design and as you design. Hold your intention. Every now and then, think of why you do what you do, what it means, what it stands for. And at the end, remain in this state, meditating for a few minutes, feeling the wonderful energy, the higher level you have entered!

STRENGTHENING THE PROCESS

There are two ways to reinforce this technique: to fill the circle with color and to add visualization.

COLOR FILLING

Fill the circle with the color green. Color inside the circle line, slowly and calmly, filling in the white area, and covering your name. You do this so as to fill the space with energy. Your aura and your body. It's like filling your body with color, with energy, with the quality you want – in this case, Health!

Think about what you are doing. Have a clear intention in your mind as you fill the circle with color:

"I fill myself with health, with the energy of health.
My aura, my energy, my body, is filled with health, with the energy of health!

Health everywhere around me and everywhere inside me...
Health everywhere around me and everywhere inside me...
Health everywhere around me and everywhere inside me... "

Or you can use your own words.

Color and fill the whole circle.

You can also fill the space between the first and second circle and between the second and third circle as well, although this is not so important. Do it though, if you feel like it.

Since you have covered your name with color and you can no longer see it, rewrite it down below, below the circles, at the bottom of the paper.

VISUALIZATION

If you want to see more immediate results, add visualization into the process. You can do it at the beginning or at the end. Or twice, both at the beginning and at the end. This empowers the process to the highest degree!

Gently close your eyes, take some slow and deep breaths, and then let go. Relax your body and mind.

Visualize the circle of health around you. You can envision a green, white, or golden circle. Or of some other color. You can also visualize a sphere – this is even better! A green healing sphere around you. Or a golden sphere of health around you.

The golden sphere is the highest energy – it is all-inclusive! It is the most intelligent and wise and the strongest and most powerful energy. It is like the sun.

Feel that the sphere is full of energy, light, and power. Full of health. And you are inside it! You can see or feel this energy as green energy or as white or golden. In all cases, white or golden energy is ideal. White is the energy of life and it includes everything, all possibilities, while golden is the energy of Spirit and consciousness, of the Supreme Source and it symbolizes the infinite and perfect wisdom, love, and power of the absolute.

You are in the sphere of health, within the energy of health!

Mentally, state (or use your own words):

"I am in the sphere of health, within the energy of health.
The energy of health surrounds me; it is all around me.
And the energy of health is inside me, it is everywhere inside me.
Supreme health!
Perfect health!
Absolute health!
Health on all levels!"

You do not have to make a second or third circle or a second or third sphere. For the visualization, one circle or one sphere is enough. If, nonetheless, you feel guided to visualize more circles or spheres, go on and do it.

Finally, give thanks from your heart with the utmost love, joy, and gratitude! Open your eyes.

The highest, the most perfect health, with infinite love and unlimited joy!

PEACE AND TRANQUILITY

Take some sheets of white paper and a blue marker.

Sit comfortably and relax.

Take a few deep breaths, at a calm and slow pace. Inhale from the nose, slowly and deeply, taking your breath deep down into your belly and lower abdomen. Breathe out from the mouth, blowing the air gently, steadily, and slowly. Do these full, conscious, energetic breaths. They will release any tension, pressure, and burden and will fill you with energy, liveliness, and positivity.

Then, simply relax, and calm down your mind and body totally. Let go, let go completely.

Feel joy and have a wonderful sense of joyful anticipation, thinking about what you are going to do! You are going to give peace and tranquility to yourself, you are going to place your personal energy within greater peace and tranquility – spiritual and energetic peace and tranquility! You are about to bring forth and experience perfect peace and tranquility, total peace and tranquility, peace and tranquility on all levels!

Take the marker and one sheet of paper and write your name in the center of the paper. Your forename and then your sur-

name under it. You can write your official, complete name or the one you use in your daily encounters. You can also use your middle name, if you have one. Simply write it under your forename and above your surname.

You can also just write the initials of your forename and surname. You can even not write down your name at all. Instead, you may write or draw something on the paper that represents/symbolizes you. For instance, you can make a dot, draw a star, or a human stick figure, as a symbol for yourself. What you have in mind – your intention – is the primary and most important element in this work and the design is secondary; it is merely symbolic.

Think that, while using the marker and drawing a circle around your name, this circle symbolizes the energy and the quality you want to bring forth and experience. The ideal state/condition you want to experience. In this case, it is Peace and Tranquility.

Draw the circle around your complete name. Do it slowly, meditatively. It does not matter how large the circle is – as long as it encircles your name, that is, until it includes you. It does not have to be a perfect circle; it can be clumsy. Also, it does not matter whether you draw the circle in a left or right direction.

Do it slowly and think that what you do has great power, great power in energetic and spiritual terms.

Keep your intention in mind while you draw the circle. What does it mean? Why are you doing this?
Affirm it, either mentally or out loud:

"I create a circle of peace and tranquility around me...
A circle of peace and tranquility, around me...
I place myself within a circle of peace and tranquility...
Myself, within peace and tranquility...
I am within peace and tranquility..."

You can also repeat the quality/energy:

"Peace and tranquility... Peace and tranquility... Peace and tranquility..."

Or you can repeat both affirmations:

"Peace and tranquility... Peace and tranquility... Peace and tranquility...
I create a circle of peace and tranquility around me...
A circle of peace and tranquility around me...
I place myself within a circle of peace and tranquility...
Myself, within peace and tranquility...
I am within peace and tranquility..."

There is no right or wrong in doing this. Do it in your own way, using your own creativity, inner guidance, and intuition. You may use your own wording, affirm it in your own way. Just have a clear intention: in this case, Peace and Tranquility.

Repeat and draw the circle over and over with this color, repeating the thoughts, making adjustments, and enhancing them, making the color of the circle more intense, vivid, and uniform. Each time, re-affirm your intention for peace and tranquility.

Then, pause for a while and look at the circle and think once more what it stands for, what it means. Do you feel the energy? Relax and notice. You can also take some slow, full, deep breaths.

You can enhance and empower this energy even more!

Using the same blue color, design a second larger circle around the first one. Think of what this second larger circle means:

"Greater peace and tranquility around me...
Myself, within greater peace and tranquility...
I am in greater peace and tranquility...
More peace and tranquility...
Even more peace and tranquility...
Much more peace and tranquility...
Around myself and me in the center of it..."

Keep moving the marker around, making the circle bolder and stronger. Do it in a steady, slow, and meditative manner. Keep the above statement in your mind or repeat it out loud. Once more, you can use your own words but focus on your intention for even greater peace and tranquility.

Make another pause and observe the drawing, and notice how you feel its energy. It works, it starts to manifest! It is manifesting its effects and it is powerful! You can also take some more deep, slow, full breaths.

Now let's take this to the maximum, to its greatest height and power.

Make a third, even larger circle, around the second one. Again, in the color blue. It symbolizes the highest possible level of energy, the greatest possible peace and tranquility! Absolute, perfect, total, divine peace and tranquility! Peace and tranquility on all levels!

Think about this meaning, as you draw the circle, slowly and meditatively. Repeat the circle a few times, over and over, and each time, think or say out loud the following:

"Perfect peace and tranquility around me...
Myself, in perfect peace and tranquility...
I am within perfect peace and tranquility...
The highest level of peace and tranquility!
The greatest, the supreme peace and tranquility!
Absolute and perfect peace and tranquility!
Total and complete peace and tranquility!
Peace and tranquility on all levels!"

As always, you can use your own wording, keeping in mind your intention for the highest level of this energy, the greatest possible peace and tranquility.

Stop and relax once more, noticing and observing everything. Feel the amazing energy and power! Stay for a few moments in this high positive state, receiving and experiencing all that goodness! You can also take some more deep, slow, full breaths.

For this third circle, the third level of this work, you can also use a different color, a golden one. The color gold symbolizes the golden light, the highest spiritual light. The highest level of energy and the highest level of consciousness; super-consciousness, spiritual or divine consciousness. The golden light is the light of Spirit, the Logos, and the Source/the Absolute. It is pure wisdom, pure love, and pure power... infinite wisdom – infinite love – infinite power and perfect wisdom – perfect love – perfect power!

This technique can be done using other colors too. Instead of the blue color, you may use any color you want. You could also make more circles, as many as you want. You control and define what it is that you do, what energy/quality you create, and in what way. Just be aware, know what it is that you're doing, why you are doing each move, the purpose behind each thing.

For example, you can use all the colors, symbolizing different aspects and qualities of peace and tranquility, or meaning peace and tranquility on different levels and for different areas of your life.

Try both: peace and tranquility with a variety of different colors and peace and tranquility using only the blue color, or with a combination of blue and gold at the end.

You can do just one circle. Leave the drawing as it is and then, after some time has passed or even days later, add a second circle or a third one. Once again, there is no right or wrong; you will be guided. Maybe you make many circles, then decide they are not needed, and so you do the process again, with just one circle this time. Follow your intuition.

Make the process esoterically, calmly, meditatively, and make pauses to feel the energy. Take deep breaths at the beginning and at the end of this exercise and during its practice. Focus on your purpose, clarify your intention, before you begin to design and as you design. Hold your intention. Every now and then, think of why you do what you do, what it means, what it stands for. And at the end, remain in this state, meditating for a few minutes, feeling the wonderful energy, the higher level you have entered!

STRENGTHENING THE PROCESS

There are two ways to reinforce this technique: to fill the circle with color and to add visualization.

COLOR FILLING

Fill the circle with the color blue. Color inside the circle line, slowly and calmly, filling in the white area, and covering your name. You do this so as to fill the space with energy. Your aura and your body. It's like filling your body with color, with energy, with the quality you want – in this case, Peace and Tranquility!

Think about what you are doing. Have a clear intention in your mind as you fill the circle with color:

"I fill myself with peace and tranquility, with the energy of peace and tranquility.
My aura, my energy, my body, is filled with peace and tranquility, with the energy of peace and tranquility!
Peace and tranquility everywhere around me and everywhere inside me...
Peace and tranquility everywhere around me and everywhere inside me...
Peace and tranquility everywhere around me and everywhere inside me... "

Or you can use your own words.

Color and fill the whole circle.

You can also fill the space between the first and second circle and between the second and third circle as well, although this is not so important. Do it though, if you feel like it.

Since you have covered your name with color and you can no longer see it, rewrite it down below, below the circles, at the bottom of the paper.

VISUALIZATION

If you want to see more immediate results, add visualization into the process. You can do it at the beginning or at the end.

Or twice, both at the beginning and at the end. This empowers the process to the highest degree!

Gently close your eyes, take some slow and deep breaths, and then let go. Relax your body and mind.

Visualize the circle of peace and tranquility around you. You can envision a blue, white, or golden circle. Or of some other color. You can also visualize a sphere – this is even better! A blue sphere of peace and tranquility around you. Or a golden sphere of peace and tranquility around you. The golden sphere is the highest energy – it is all-inclusive! It is the most intelligent and wise and the strongest and most powerful energy. It is like the sun.

Feel that the sphere is full of energy, light, and power. Full of peace and tranquility. And you are inside it! You can see or feel this energy as blue energy or as white or golden. In all cases, white or golden energy is ideal. White is the energy of life and it includes everything, all possibilities, while golden is the energy of Spirit and consciousness, of the Supreme Source and it symbolizes the infinite and perfect wisdom, love, and power of the absolute.

You are in the sphere of peace and tranquility, within the energy of peace and tranquility!

Mentally, state (or use your own words):

"I am in the sphere of peace and tranquility, within the energy of peace and tranquility.

The energy of peace and tranquility surrounds me; it is all around me.

And the energy of peace and tranquility is inside me, it is everywhere inside me.
Supreme peace and tranquility!
Perfect peace and tranquility!
Absolute peace and tranquility!
Peace and tranquility on all levels!"

You do not have to make a second or third circle or a second or third sphere. For the visualization, one circle or one sphere is enough. If, nonetheless, you feel guided to visualize more circles or spheres, go on and do it.

Finally, give thanks from your heart with the utmost love, joy, and gratitude! Open your eyes.

The highest, the most perfect peace and tranquility, with infinite love and unlimited joy!

JOY AND BLISS

Take some sheets of white paper and an orange marker.

Sit comfortably and relax.

Take a few deep breaths, at a calm and slow pace. Inhale from the nose, slowly and deeply, taking your breath deep down into your belly and lower abdomen. Breathe out from the mouth, blowing the air gently, steadily, and slowly. Do these full, conscious, energetic breaths. They will release any tension, pressure, and burden and will fill you with energy, liveliness, and positivity.

Then, simply relax, and calm down your mind and body totally. Let go, let go completely.

Feel joy and have a wonderful sense of joyful anticipation, thinking about what you are going to do! You are going to give joy and bliss to yourself, you are going to place your personal energy within greater joy and bliss – spiritual and energetic joy and bliss! You are about to bring forth and experience perfect joy and bliss, total joy and bliss, joy and bliss on all levels!

Take the marker and one sheet of paper and write your name in the center of the paper. Your forename and then your sur-

name under it. You can write your official, complete name or the one you use in your daily encounters. You can also use your middle name, if you have one. Simply write it under your forename and above your surname.

You can also just write the initials of your forename and surname. You can even not write down your name at all. Instead, you may write or draw something on the paper that represents/symbolizes you. For instance, you can make a dot, draw a star, or a human stick figure, as a symbol for yourself. What you have in mind – your intention – is the primary and most important element in this work and the design is secondary; it is merely symbolic.

Think that, while using the marker and drawing a circle around your name, this circle symbolizes the energy and the quality you want to bring forth and experience. The ideal state/condition you want to experience. In this case, it is Joy and Bliss.

Draw the circle around your complete name. Do it slowly, meditatively. It does not matter how large the circle is – as long as it encircles your name, that is, until it includes you. It does not have to be a perfect circle; it can be clumsy. Also, it does not matter whether you draw the circle in a left or right direction.

Do it slowly and think that what you do has great power, great power in energetic and spiritual terms.

Keep your intention in mind while you draw the circle. What does it mean? Why are you doing this?
Affirm it, either mentally or out loud:

"I create a circle of joy and bliss around me...
A circle of joy and bliss, around me...
I place myself within a circle of joy and bliss...
Myself, within joy and bliss...
I am within joy and bliss..."

You can also repeat the quality/energy:

"Joy and bliss... Joy and bliss... Joy and bliss..."

Or you can repeat both affirmations:

"Joy and bliss... Joy and bliss... Joy and bliss...
I create a circle of joy and bliss around me...
A circle of joy and bliss around me...
I place myself within a circle of joy and bliss...
Myself, within joy and bliss...
I am within joy and bliss..."

There is no right or wrong in doing this. Do it in your own way, using your own creativity, inner guidance, and intuition. You may use your own wording, affirm it in your own way. Just have a clear intention: in this case, Joy and Bliss.

Repeat and draw the circle over and over with this color, repeating the thoughts, making adjustments, and enhancing

them, making the color of the circle more intense, vivid, and uniform. Each time, re-affirm your intention for joy and bliss. Then, pause for a while and look at the circle and think once more what it stands for, what it means. Do you feel the energy? Relax and notice. You can also take some slow, full, deep breaths.

You can enhance and empower this energy even more!

Using the same orange color, design a second larger circle around the first one. Think of what this second larger circle means:

"Greater joy and bliss around me...
Myself, within greater joy and bliss...
I am in greater joy and bliss...
More joy and bliss...
Even more joy and bliss...
Much more joy and bliss...
Around myself and me in the center of it..."

Keep moving the marker around, making the circle bolder and stronger. Do it in a steady, slow, and meditative manner. Keep the above statement in your mind or repeat it out loud. Once more, you can use your own words but focus on your intention for even greater joy and bliss.

Make another pause and observe the drawing, and notice how you feel its energy. It works, it starts to manifest! It is manifesting its effects and it is powerful! You can also take some more deep, slow, full breaths.

Now let's take this to the maximum, to its greatest height and power.

Make a third, even larger circle, around the second one. Again, in the color orange. It symbolizes the highest possible level of energy, the greatest possible joy and bliss! Absolute, perfect, total, divine joy and bliss! Joy and bliss on all levels!

Think about this meaning, as you draw the circle, slowly and meditatively. Repeat the circle a few times, over and over, and each time, think or say out loud the following:

"Perfect joy and bliss around me...
Myself, in perfect joy and bliss...
I am within perfect joy and bliss...
The highest level of joy and bliss!
The greatest, the supreme joy and bliss!
Absolute and perfect joy and bliss!
Total and complete joy and bliss!
Joy and bliss on all levels!"

As always, you can use your own wording, keeping in mind your intention for the highest level of this energy, the greatest possible joy and bliss.

Stop and relax once more, noticing and observing everything. Feel the amazing energy and power! Stay for a few moments in this high positive state, receiving and experiencing all that goodness! You can also take some more deep, slow, full breaths.

For this third circle, the third level of this work, you can also use a different color, a golden one. The color gold symbolizes the golden light, the highest spiritual light. The highest level of energy and the highest level of consciousness; super-consciousness, spiritual or divine consciousness. The golden light is the light of Spirit, the Logos, and the Source/the Absolute. It is pure wisdom, pure love, and pure power... infinite wisdom – infinite love – infinite power and perfect wisdom – perfect love – perfect power!

This technique can be done using other colors too. Instead of the orange color, you may use any color you want. You could also make more circles, as many as you want. You control and define what it is that you do, what energy/quality you create, and in what way. Just be aware, know what it is that you're doing, why you are doing each move, the purpose behind each thing.

For example, you can use all the colors, symbolizing different aspects and qualities of joy and bliss, or meaning joy and bliss on different levels and for different areas of your life.

Try both: joy and bliss with a variety of diffcrent colors and joy and bliss using only the orange color, or with a combination of orange and gold at the end.

You can do just one circle. Leave the drawing as it is and then, after some time has passed or even days later, add a second circle or a third one. Once again, there is no right or wrong; you will be guided. Maybe you make many circles, then decide they are not needed, and so you do the process again, with just one circle this time. Follow your intuition.

Make the process esoterically, calmly, meditatively, and make pauses to feel the energy. Take deep breaths at the beginning and at the end of this exercise and during its practice. Focus on your purpose, clarify your intention, before you begin to design and as you design. Hold your intention. Every now and then, think of why you do what you do, what it means, what it stands for. And at the end, remain in this state, meditating for a few minutes, feeling the wonderful energy, the higher level you have entered!

STRENGTHENING THE PROCESS

There are two ways to reinforce this technique: to fill the circle with color and to add visualization.

COLOR FILLING

Fill the circle with the color orange. Color inside the circle line, slowly and calmly, filling in the white area, and covering your name. You do this so as to fill the space with energy. Your aura and your body. It's like filling your body with color, with energy, with the quality you want – in this case, Joy and Bliss!

Think about what you are doing. Have a clear intention in your mind as you fill the circle with color:
"I fill myself with joy and bliss, with the energy of joy and bliss. My aura, my energy, my body, is filled with joy and bliss, with the energy of joy and bliss!

Joy and bliss everywhere around me and everywhere inside me...
Joy and bliss everywhere around me and everywhere inside me...
Joy and bliss everywhere around me and everywhere inside me... "

Or you can use your own words.

Color and fill the whole circle.

You can also fill the space between the first and second circle and between the second and third circle as well, although this is not so important. Do it though, if you feel like it.

Since you have covered your name with color and you can no longer see it, rewrite it down below, below the circles, at the bottom of the paper.

VISUALIZATION

If you want to see more immediate results, add visualization into the process. You can do it at the beginning or at the end. Or twice, both at the beginning and at the end. This empowers the process to the highest degree!

Gently close your eyes, take some slow and deep breaths, and then let go. Relax your body and mind.

Visualize the circle of joy and bliss around you. You can envision an orange, white, or golden circle. Or of some other color.

You can also visualize a sphere – this is even better! An orange sphere of joy and bliss around you. Or a golden sphere of joy and bliss around you. The golden sphere is the highest energy – it is all-inclusive! It is the most intelligent and wise and the strongest and most powerful energy. It is like the sun.

Feel that the sphere is full of energy, light, and power. Full of joy and bliss. And you are inside it! You can see or feel this energy as orange energy or as white or golden. In all cases, white or golden energy is ideal. White is the energy of life and it includes everything, all possibilities, while golden is the energy of Spirit and consciousness, of the Supreme Source and it symbolizes the infinite and perfect wisdom, love, and power of the absolute.

You are in the sphere of joy and bliss, within the energy of joy and bliss!

Mentally, state (or use your own words):

"I am in the sphere of joy and bliss, within the energy of joy and bliss.
The energy of joy and bliss surrounds me; it is all around me.
And the energy of joy and bliss is inside me, it is everywhere inside me.
Supreme joy and bliss!
Perfect joy and bliss!
Absolute joy and bliss!
Joy and bliss on all levels!"

You do not have to make a second or third circle or a second or third sphere. For the visualization, one circle or one sphere is enough. If, nonetheless, you feel guided to visualize more circles or spheres, go on and do it.

Finally, give thanks from your heart with the utmost love, joy, and gratitude! Open your eyes.

The highest, the most perfect joy and bliss, with infinite love and unlimited joy!

ABUNDANCE AND PROSPERITY

Take some sheets of white paper and a red marker.

Sit comfortably and relax.

Take a few deep breaths, at a calm and slow pace. Inhale from the nose, slowly and deeply, taking your breath deep down into your belly and lower abdomen. Breathe out from the mouth, blowing the air gently, steadily, and slowly. Do these full, conscious, energetic breaths. They will release any tension, pressure, and burden and will fill you with energy, liveliness, and positivity.

Then, simply relax, and calm down your mind and body totally. Let go, let go completely.

Feel joy and have a wonderful sense of joyful anticipation, thinking about what you are going to do! You are going to give abundance and prosperity to yourself, you are going to place your personal energy within greater abundance and prosperity – spiritual and energetic abundance and prosperity! You are about to bring forth and experience perfect abundance and prosperity, total abundance and prosperity, abundance and prosperity on all levels!

Take the marker and one sheet of paper and write your name

in the center of the paper. Your forename and then your surname under it. You can write your official, complete name or the one you use in your daily encounters. You can also use your middle name, if you have one. Simply write it under your forename and above your surname.

You can also just write the initials of your forename and surname. You can even not write down your name at all. Instead, you may write or draw something on the paper that represents/symbolizes you. For instance, you can make a dot, draw a star, or a human stick figure, as a symbol for yourself. What you have in mind – your intention – is the primary and most important element in this work and the design is secondary; it is merely symbolic.

Think that, while using the marker and drawing a circle around your name, this circle symbolizes the energy and the quality you want to bring forth and experience. The ideal state/condition you want to experience. In this case, it is Abundance and Prosperity.

Draw the circle around your complete name. Do it slowly, meditatively. It does not matter how large the circle is – as long as it encircles your name, that is, until it includes you. It does not have to be a perfect circle; it can be clumsy. Also, it does not matter whether you draw the circle in a left or right direction.

Do it slowly and think that what you do has great power, great power in energetic and spiritual terms.

Keep your intention in mind while you draw the circle. What does it mean? Why are you doing this?
Affirm it, either mentally or out loud:

"I create a circle of abundance and prosperity around me...
A circle of abundance and prosperity, around me...
I place myself within a circle of abundance and prosperity...
Myself, within abundance and prosperity...
I am within abundance and prosperity..."

You can also repeat the quality/energy:

"Abundance and prosperity... Abundance and prosperity... Abundance and prosperity..."

Or you can repeat both affirmations:

"Abundance and prosperity... Abundance and prosperity... Abundance and prosperity...
I create a circle of abundance and prosperity around me...
A circle of abundance and prosperity around me...
I place myself within a circle of abundance and prosperity...
Myself, within abundance and prosperity...
I am within abundance and prosperity..."

There is no right or wrong in doing this. Do it in your own way, using your own creativity, inner guidance, and intuition. You may use your own wording, affirm it in your own way. Just have a clear intention: in this case, Abundance and Prosperity.

Repeat and draw the circle over and over with this color, repeating the thoughts, making adjustments, and enhancing them, making the color of the circle more intense, vivid, and uniform. Each time, re-affirm your intention for abundance and prosperity.

Then, pause for a while and look at the circle and think once more what it stands for, what it means. Do you feel the energy? Relax and notice. You can also take some slow, full, deep breaths.

You can enhance and empower this energy even more!

Using the same red color, design a second larger circle around the first one. Think of what this second larger circle means:

"Greater abundance and prosperity around me...
Myself, within greater abundance and prosperity...
I am in greater abundance and prosperity...
More abundance and prosperity...
Even more abundance and prosperity...
Much more abundance and prosperity...
Around myself and me in the center of it..."

Keep moving the marker around, making the circle bolder and stronger. Do it in a steady, slow, and meditative manner. Keep the above statement in your mind or repeat it out loud. Once more, you can use your own words but focus on your intention for even greater abundance and prosperity.

Make another pause and observe the drawing, and notice how you feel its energy. It works, it starts to manifest! It is manifesting its effects and it is powerful! You can also take some more deep, slow, full breaths.

Now let's take this to the maximum, to its greatest height and power.

Make a third, even larger circle, around the second one. Again, in the color red. It symbolizes the highest possible level of energy, the greatest possible abundance and prosperity! Absolute, perfect, total, divine abundance and prosperity! Abundance and prosperity on all levels!

Think about this meaning, as you draw the circle, slowly and meditatively. Repeat the circle a few times, over and over, and each time, think or say out loud the following:

"Perfect abundance and prosperity around me...
Myself, in perfect abundance and prosperity...
I am within perfect abundance and prosperity...
The highest level of abundance and prosperity!
The greatest, the supreme abundance and prosperity!
Absolute and perfect abundance and prosperity!
Total and complete abundance and prosperity!
Abundance and prosperity on all levels!"

As always, you can use your own wording, keeping in mind your intention for the highest level of this energy, the greatest possible abundance and prosperity.

Stop and relax once more, noticing and observing everything. Feel the amazing energy and power! Stay for a few moments in this high positive state, receiving and experiencing all that goodness! You can also take some more deep, slow, full breaths.

For this third circle, the third level of this work, you can also use a different color, a golden one. The color gold symbolizes the golden light, the highest spiritual light. The highest level of energy and the highest level of consciousness; super-consciousness, spiritual or divine consciousness. The golden light is the light of Spirit, the Logos, and the Source/the Absolute. It is pure wisdom, pure love, and pure power... infinite wisdom – infinite love – infinite power and perfect wisdom – perfect love – perfect power!

This technique can be done using other colors too. Instead of the red color, you may use any color you want. You could also make more circles, as many as you want. You control and define what it is that you do, what energy/quality you create, and in what way. Just be aware, know what it is that you're doing, why you are doing each move, the purpose behind each thing.

For example, you can use all the colors, symbolizing different aspects and qualities of abundance and prosperity, or meaning abundance and prosperity on different levels and for different areas of your life.

Try both: abundance and prosperity with a variety of different colors and abundance and prosperity using only the red color, or with a combination of red and gold at the end.

You can do just one circle. Leave the drawing as it is and then, after some time has passed or even days later, add a second circle or a third one. Once again, there is no right or wrong; you will be guided. Maybe you make many circles, then decide they are not needed, and so you do the process again, with just one circle this time. Follow your intuition.

Make the process esoterically, calmly, meditatively, and make pauses to feel the energy. Take deep breaths at the beginning and at the end of this exercise and during its practice. Focus on your purpose, clarify your intention, before you begin to design and as you design. Hold your intention. Every now and then, think of why you do what you do, what it means, what it stands for. And at the end, remain in this state, meditating for a few minutes, feeling the wonderful energy, the higher level you have entered!

STRENGTHENING THE PROCESS

There are two ways to reinforce this technique: to fill the circle with color and to add visualization.

COLOR FILLING

Fill the circle with the color red. Color inside the circle line, slowly and calmly, filling in the white area, and covering your name. You do this so as to fill the space with energy. Your aura and your body. It's like filling your body with color, with energy, with the quality you want – in this case, Abundance and Prosperity!

Think about what you are doing. Have a clear intention in your mind as you fill the circle with color:

"I fill myself with abundance and prosperity, with the energy of abundance and prosperity.
My aura, my energy, my body, is filled with abundance and prosperity, with the energy of abundance and prosperity!
Abundance and prosperity everywhere around me and everywhere inside me...
Abundance and prosperity everywhere around me and everywhere inside me...
Abundance and prosperity everywhere around me and everywhere inside me... "

Or you can use your own words.

Color and fill the whole circle.

You can also fill the space between the first and second circle and between the second and third circle as well, although this is not so important. Do it though, if you feel like it.

Since you have covered your name with color and you can no longer see it, rewrite it down below, below the circles, at the bottom of the paper.

VISUALIZATION

If you want to see more immediate results, add visualization into the process. You can do it at the beginning or at the end. Or twice, both at the beginning and at the end. This empowers the process to the highest degree!

Gently close your eyes, take some slow and deep breaths, and then let go. Relax your body and mind.

Visualize the circle of abundance and prosperity around you. You can envision a red, white, or golden circle. Or of some other color. You can also visualize a sphere – this is even better! A red sphere of abundance and prosperity around you. Or a golden sphere of abundance and prosperity around you. The golden sphere is the highest energy – it is all-inclusive! It is the most intelligent and wise and the strongest and most powerful energy. It is like the sun.

Feel that the sphere is full of energy, light, and power. Full of abundance and prosperity. And you are inside it! You can see or feel this energy as red energy or as white or golden. In all cases, white or golden energy is ideal. White is the energy of life and it includes everything, all possibilities, while golden is the energy of Spirit and consciousness, of the Supreme Source and it symbolizes the infinite and perfect wisdom, love, and power of the absolute.

You are in the sphere of abundance and prosperity, within the energy of abundance and prosperity!

Mentally, state (or use your own words):

"I am in the sphere of abundance and prosperity, within the energy of abundance and prosperity.
The energy of abundance and prosperity surrounds me; it is all around me.
And the energy of abundance and prosperity is inside me, it is everywhere inside me.
Supreme abundance and prosperity!
Perfect abundance and prosperity!
Absolute abundance and prosperity!
Abundance and prosperity on all levels!"

You do not have to make a second or third circle or a second or third sphere. For the visualization, one circle or one sphere is enough. If, nonetheless, you feel guided to visualize more circles or spheres, go on and do it.

Finally, give thanks from your heart with the utmost love, joy, and gratitude! Open your eyes.

The highest, the most perfect abundance and prosperity, with infinite love and unlimited joy!

A LOVING ROMANTIC RELATIONSHIP

Take some sheets of white paper and a red marker.

Sit comfortably and relax.

Take a few deep breaths, at a calm and slow pace. Inhale from the nose, slowly and deeply, taking your breath deep down into your belly and lower abdomen. Breathe out from the mouth, blowing the air gently, steadily, and slowly. Do these full, conscious, energetic breaths. They will release any tension, pressure, and burden and will fill you with energy, liveliness, and positivity.

Then, simply relax, and calm down your mind and body totally. Let go, let go completely.

Feel joy and have a wonderful sense of joyful anticipation, thinking about what you are going to do! You are going to give yourself the energy for a loving romantic relationship, you are going to place your personal energy within a loving romantic relationship – the spiritual and energetic state of a loving romantic relationship! You are about to bring forth and experience a higher loving romantic relationship, a deeper loving romantic relationship, a perfect and ideal romantic relationship on all levels!

Take the marker and one sheet of paper and write your name in the center of the paper. Your forename and then your surname under it. You can write your official, complete name or the one you use in your daily encounters. You can also use your middle name, if you have one. Simply write it under your forename and above your surname.

You can also just write the initials of your forename and surname. You can even not write down your name at all. Instead, you may write or draw something on the paper that represents/symbolizes you. For instance, you can make a dot, draw a star, or a human stick figure, as a symbol for yourself. What you have in mind – your intention – is the primary and most important element in this work and the design is secondary; it is merely symbolic.

Think that, while using the marker and drawing a circle around your name, this circle symbolizes the energy and the quality you want to bring forth and experience. The ideal state/condition you want to experience. In this case, it is a Loving Romantic Relationship.

Draw the circle around your complete name and surname. Do it slowly, meditatively. It does not matter how large the circle is – as long as it encircles your name, that is, until it includes you. It does not have to be a perfect circle, it can be clumsy. Also, it does not matter whether you draw the circle in a left or right direction.

Do it slowly and think that what you do has great power, great power in energetic and spiritual terms.

Keep your intention in mind while you draw the circle. What does it mean? Why are you doing this?

Affirm it, either mentally or out loud:

"I create a circle of a loving romantic relationship around me...
A circle of a loving romantic relationship, around me...
I place myself within a circle of a loving romantic relationship...
Myself, within a loving romantic relationship...
I am within a loving romantic relationship..."

You can also repeat the quality/energy:

"A loving romantic relationship... A loving romantic relationship... A loving romantic relationship..."

Or you can repeat both affirmations:

"A loving romantic relationship... A loving romantic relationship... A loving romantic relationship...
I create a circle of a loving romantic relationship around me...
A circle of a loving romantic relationship around me...
I place myself within a circle of a loving romantic relationship...
Myself, within a loving romantic relationship...
I am within a loving romantic relationship..."

There is no right or wrong in doing this. Do it in your own way, using your own creativity, inner guidance, and intuition.

You may use your own wording, affirm it in your own way. Just have a clear intention: in this case, a Loving Romantic Relationship.

Repeat and draw the circle over and over with this color, repeating the thoughts, making adjustments, and enhancing them, making the color of the circle more intense, vivid, and uniform. Each time, re-affirm your intention for a loving romantic relationship.

Then, pause for a while and look at the circle and think once more what it stands for, what it means. Do you feel the energy? Relax and notice. You can also take some slow, full, deep breaths.

You can enhance and empower this energy even more!

Using the same red color, design a second larger circle around the first one. Think of what this second larger circle means:

"A greater loving romantic relationship around me...
Myself, within a greater loving romantic relationship...
I am in a greater loving romantic relationship...
A more loving romantic relationship...
An even more loving romantic relationship...
A much more loving romantic relationship...
Around myself and me in the center of it..."

Keep moving the marker around, making the circle bolder and stronger. Do it in a steady, slow, and meditative manner. Keep the above statement in your mind or repeat it out loud. Once more, you can use your own words but focus on your intention for an even greater loving romantic relationship.

Make another pause and observe the drawing and notice how you feel its energy. It works, it starts to manifest! It is manifesting its effects and it is powerful! You can also take some more deep, slow, full breaths.

Now let's take this to the maximum, to its greatest height and power.

Make a third, even larger circle, around the second one. Again, in the color red. It symbolizes the highest possible level of energy, the greatest possible loving romantic relationship! Absolute, perfect, total, divine loving romantic relationship! A most loving romantic relationship on all levels!

Think about this meaning, as you draw the circle, slowly and meditatively. Repeat the circle a few times, over and over, and each time, think or say out loud the following:

"A perfect loving romantic relationship around me...
Myself, in a perfect loving romantic relationship...
I am within a perfect loving romantic relationship...
The highest level of a loving romantic relationship!
The greatest, the supreme loving romantic relationship!
An absolute and perfect loving romantic relationship!
A total and complete loving romantic relationship!
The most loving romantic relationship on all levels!"

As always, you can use your own wording, keeping in mind your intention for the highest level of this energy, the greatest possible loving romantic relationship.

Stop and relax once more, noticing and observing everything. Feel the amazing energy and power! Stay for a few moments in this high positive state, receiving and experiencing all that goodness! You can also take some more deep, slow, full breaths.

For this third circle, the third level of this work, you can also use a different color, a golden one. The color gold symbolizes the golden light, the highest spiritual light. The highest level of energy and the highest level of consciousness; super-consciousness, spiritual or divine consciousness. The golden light is the light of Spirit, the Logos, and the Source/the Absolute. It is pure wisdom, pure love, and pure power... infinite wisdom – infinite love – infinite power and perfect wisdom – perfect love – perfect power!

This technique can be done using other colors too. Instead of the red color, you may use any color you want. You could also make more circles, as many as you want. You control and define what it is that you do, what energy/quality you create, and in what way. Just be aware, know what it is that you're doing, why you are doing each move, the purpose behind each thing.

For example, you can use all the colors, symbolizing different aspects and qualities of a loving romantic relationship.

Try both; a loving romantic relationship with a variety of different colors and a loving romantic relationship using only the red color or with a combination of red and gold at the end.

You can do just one circle. Leave the drawing as it is and then, after some time has passed or even days later, add a second circle or a third one. Once again, there is no right or wrong; you will be guided. Maybe you make many circles, then decide they are not needed, and so you do the process again, with just one circle this time. Follow your intuition.

Make the process esoterically, calmly, meditatively, and make pauses to feel the energy. Take deep breaths at the beginning and at the end of this exercise and during its practice. Focus on your purpose, clarify your intention, before you begin to design and as you design. Hold your intention. Every now and then, think of why you do what you do, what it means, what it stands for. And at the end, remain in this state, meditating for a few minutes, feeling the wonderful energy, the higher level you have entered!

STRENGTHENING THE PROCESS

There are two ways to reinforce this technique: to fill the circle with color and to add visualization.

COLOR FILLING

Fill the circle with the color red. Color inside the circle line, slowly and calmly, filling in the white area, and covering your name. You do this so as to fill the space with energy. Your aura and your body. It's like filling your body with color, with energy, with the quality you want – in this case, a Loving Romantic Relationship!

Think about what you are doing. Have a clear intention in your mind as you fill the circle with color:

"I fill myself with the energy of a loving romantic relationship, with the energy of the most loving romantic relationship.
My aura, my energy, my body, is filled with the energy of a loving romantic relationship, with the energy of the most loving romantic relationship!
A loving romantic relationship everywhere around me and everywhere inside me...
A loving romantic relationship everywhere around me and everywhere inside me...
A loving romantic relationship everywhere around me and everywhere inside me... "

Or you can use your own words.

Color and fill the whole circle.

You can also fill the space between the first and second circle and between the second and third circle as well, although this is not so important. Do it though, if you feel like it.

Since you have covered your name with color and you can no longer see it, rewrite it down below, below the circles, at the bottom of the paper.

VISUALIZATION

If you want to see more immediate results, add visualization into the process. You can do it at the beginning or at the end. Or twice, both at the beginning and at the end. This empowers the process to the highest degree!

Gently close your eyes, take some slow and deep breaths, and then let go. Relax your body and mind.

Visualize the circle of a loving romantic relationship around you. You can envision a red, white, or golden circle. Or of some other color. You can also visualize a sphere – this is even better! A red sphere of a loving romantic relationship around you. Or a golden sphere of a loving romantic relationship around you. The golden sphere is the highest energy, it is all-inclusive! It is the most intelligent and wise and the strongest and most powerful energy. It is like the sun.

Feel that the sphere is full of energy, light, and power. Full of the energy of the most loving romantic relationship. And you are inside it! You can see or feel this energy as red energy or as white or golden. In all cases, the white or golden energy is ideal. White is the energy of life and it includes everything, all possibilities, while golden is the energy of spirit and consciousness, of the Supreme Source and it symbolizes the infinite and perfect wisdom, love, and power of the absolute.

You are in the sphere of the most loving romantic relationship, within the energy of the most loving romantic relationship!

Mentally, state (or use your own words):

"I am in the sphere of a loving romantic relationship, within the energy of the most loving romantic relationship.
The energy of the most loving romantic relationship surrounds me, it is all around me.
And the energy of the most loving romantic relationship is inside me, it is everywhere inside me.
A supremely loving romantic relationship!
A perfectly loving romantic relationship!
An absolutely loving romantic relationship!
The most loving romantic relationship on all levels!"

You do not have to make a second or third circle or a second or third sphere. For the visualization, one circle or one sphere is enough. If, nonetheless, you feel guided to visualize more circles or spheres, go on and do it.

Finally, give thanks from your heart with the utmost love, joy, and gratitude! Open your eyes.

The highest, the most perfect loving romantic relationship, with infinite love and unlimited joy!

A GOOD, POSITIVE, AND HEALTHY RELATIONSHIP (HEALING OR IMPROVING A RELATIONSHIP)

Take some sheets of white paper and an orange marker.

Sit comfortably and relax.

Take a few deep breaths, at a calm and slow pace. Inhale from the nose, slowly and deeply, taking your breath deep down into your belly and lower abdomen. Breathe out from the mouth, blowing the air gently, steadily, and slowly. Do these full, conscious, energetic breaths. They will release any tension, pressure, and burden and will fill you with energy, liveliness, and positivity.

Then, simply relax, and calm down your mind and body totally. Let go, let go completely.

Feel joy and have a wonderful sense of joyful anticipation, thinking about what you are going to do! Think of a person you want to heal or improve your relationship with. You are going to create the energy for a good, positive, and healthy relationship with this person; you are going to place your personal energy within the energy of a good, positive, and healthy relationship with this person. You are about to bring forth and experience a perfectly good, positive, and healthy relationship, a totally good, positive, and healthy relationship, the best, positive, and healthy relationship on all levels!

Take the marker and one sheet of paper and write your name in the center of the paper. Your forename and then your surname under it. You can write your official, complete name or the one you use in your daily encounters. You can also use your middle name, if you have one. Simply write it under your forename and above your surname.

You can also just write the initials of your forename and surname. You can even not write down your name at all. Instead, you may write or draw something on the paper that represents/symbolizes you. For instance, you can make a dot, draw a star, or a human stick figure, as a symbol for yourself. What you have in mind – your intention – is the primary and most important element in this work and the design is secondary; it is merely symbolic.

Think that, while using the marker and drawing a circle around your name, this circle symbolizes the energy and the quality you want to bring forth and experience. The ideal state/condition you want to experience. In this case, it is a Good, Positive, and Healthy Relationship With the Individual of Your Choice.

Draw the circle around your complete name and surname. Do it slowly, meditatively. It does not matter how large the circle is – as long as it encircles your name, that is, until it includes you. It does not have to be a perfect circle, it can be clumsy.

Also, it does not matter whether you draw the circle in a left or right direction.

Do it slowly and think that what you do has great power, great power in energetic and spiritual terms.
Keep your intention in mind while you draw the circle. What does it mean? Why are you doing this?

Affirm it, either mentally or out loud:

"I create a circle of a good, positive, and healthy relationship with ...... (name the person) around me...
A circle of a good, positive, and healthy relationship with ...... (name the person), around me...
I place myself within a circle of a good, positive, and healthy relationship with ...... (name the person)...
Myself, within a good, positive, and healthy relationship with ...... (name the person)...
I am within a good, positive, and healthy relationship with ...... (name the person)..."

You can also repeat the quality/energy:

"A good, positive, and healthy relationship with ...... (name the person)... A good, positive, and healthy relationship with ...... (name the person)... A good, positive, and healthy relationship with ...... (name the person)..."

Or you can repeat both affirmations:

"A good, positive, and healthy relationship with ...... (name the person)... A good, positive, and healthy relationship with ...... (name the person)... A good, positive, and healthy relationship with ...... (name the person)...

I create a circle of a good, positive, and healthy relationship with ...... (name the person) around me...

A circle of a good, positive, and healthy relationship with ...... (name the person), around me...

I place myself within a circle of a good, positive, and healthy relationship with ...... (name the person)...

Myself, within a good, positive, and healthy relationship with ...... (name the person)...

I am within a good, positive, and healthy relationship with ...... (name the person)..."

There is no right or wrong in doing this. Do it in your own way, using your own creativity, inner guidance, and intuition. You may use your own wording, affirm it in your own way. Just have a clear intention: in this case, a Good, Positive, and Healthy Relationship.

Repeat and draw the circle over and over with this color, repeating the thoughts, making adjustments, and enhancing them, making the color of the circle more intense, vivid, and uniform. Each time, re-affirm your intention for a good, positive, and healthy relationship.

Then, pause for a while and look at the circle and think once more what it stands for, what it means. Do you feel the energy? Relax and notice. You can also take some slow, full, deep breaths.

You can enhance and empower this energy even more!

Using the same orange color, design a second larger circle around the first one. Think of what this second larger circle means:
"A better, more positive, and healthy relationship with ...... (name the person) around me...
Myself, within a better, more positive, and healthy relationship with ...... (name the person)...
I am in a better, more positive, and healthy relationship with ...... (name the person)...
A better, more positive, and healthy relationship with ...... (name the person)...
An even better, more positive, and healthy relationship with ...... (name the person)...
A much better, much more positive, and healthy relationship with ...... (name the person)...
Around myself and me in the center of it..."

Keep moving the marker around, making the circle bolder and stronger. Do it in a steady, slow, and meditative manner. Keep the above statement in your mind or repeat it out loud. Once more, you can use your own words but focus on your intention for an even better, positive, and healthy relationship.

Make another pause and observe the drawing, and notice how you feel its energy. It works, it starts to manifest! It is manifesting its effects and it is powerful! You can also take some more deep, slow, full breaths.

Now let's take this to the maximum, to its greatest height and power.

Make a third, even larger circle, around the second one. Again, in the color orange. It symbolizes the highest possible level of energy, the greatest, most positive and healthy relationship! An absolute, perfect, total, divine relationship! The greatest relationship on all levels!

Think about this meaning, as you draw the circle, slowly and meditatively. Repeat the circle a few times, over and over, and each time, think or say out loud the following:

"A perfect relationship with ...... (name the person) around me...
Myself, in a perfect relationship with ...... (name the person)...
I am within a perfect relationship with ...... (name the person)...
The highest level of a good, positive, and healthy relationship with ...... (name the person)!
The greatest, the supreme relationship with ...... (name the person)!
Absolutely good and perfectly positive relationship with ...... (name the person)!
Totally good and completely positive relationship with ...... (name the person)!
A good, positive, and healthy relationship on all levels!"

As always, you can use your own wording, keeping in mind your intention for the highest level of this energy, the greatest possible, positive, and healthy relationship.

Stop and relax once more, noticing and observing everything. Feel the amazing energy and power! Stay for a few moments in this high positive state, receiving and experiencing all that goodness! You can also take some more deep, slow, full breaths.

For this third circle, the third level of this work, you can also use a different color, a golden one. The color gold symbolizes the golden light, the highest spiritual light. The highest level of energy and the highest level of consciousness; super-consciousness, spiritual or divine consciousness. The golden light is the light of Spirit, the Logos, and the Source/the Absolute. It is pure wisdom, pure love, and pure power... infinite wisdom – infinite love – infinite power and perfect wisdom – perfect love – perfect power!

This technique can be done using other colors too. Instead of the orange color, you may use any color you want. You could also make more circles, as many as you want. You control and define what it is that you do, what energy/quality you create, and in what way. Just be aware, know what it is that you're doing, why you are doing each move, the purpose behind each thing.

For example, you can use all the colors, symbolizing different aspects and qualities of a good, positive, and healthy relationship or meaning a good, positive, and healthy relationship on different levels.

Try both; a good, positive, and healthy relationship with a variety of different colors and a good, positive, and healthy relationship using only the orange color or with a combination of orange and gold at the end.

You can do just one circle. Leave the drawing as it is and then, after some time has passed or even days later, add a second circle or a third one. Once again, there is no right or wrong; you will be guided. Maybe you make many circles, then decide they are not needed, and so you do the process again, with just one circle this time. Follow your intuition.

Make the process esoterically, calmly, meditatively, and make pauses to feel the energy. Take deep breaths at the beginning and at the end of this exercise and during its practice. Focus on your purpose, clarify your intention, before you begin to design and as you design. Hold your intention. Every now and then, think of why you do what you do, what it means, what it stands for. And at the end, remain in this state, meditating for a few minutes, feeling the wonderful energy, the higher level you have entered!

STRENGTHENING THE PROCESS

There are two ways to reinforce this technique: to fill the circle with color and to add visualization.

COLOR FILLING

Fill the circle with the color orange. Color inside the circle line, slowly and calmly, filling in the white area, and covering your name. You do this so as to fill the space with energy. Your aura and your body. It's like filling your body with color, with energy, with the quality you want – in this case, a Good, Positive, and Healthy Relationship!

Think about what you are doing. Have a clear intention in your mind as you fill the circle with color:

"I fill myself with the energy of a good, positive, and healthy relationship with ...... (name the person).
My aura, my energy, my body, is filled with the energy of a good, positive, and healthy relationship with ...... (name the person).
A good, positive, and healthy relationship with ...... (name the person) everywhere around me and everywhere inside me...
A good, positive, and healthy relationship with ...... (name the person) everywhere around me and everywhere inside me...
A good, positive, and healthy relationship with ...... (name the person) everywhere around me and everywhere inside me... "

Or you can use your own words.

Color and fill the whole circle.

You can also fill the space between the first and second circle and between the second and third circle as well, although this is not so important. Do it though, if you feel like it.

Since you have covered your name with color and you can no

longer see it, rewrite it down below, below the circles, at the bottom of the paper.

VISUALIZATION

If you want to see more immediate results, add visualization into the process. You can do it at the beginning or at the end. Or twice, both at the beginning and at the end. This empowers the process to the highest degree!

Gently close your eyes, take some slow and deep breaths, and then let go. Relax your body and mind.

Visualize the circle of a good, positive, and healthy relationship around you. You can envision an orange, white, or golden circle. Or of some other color. You can also visualize a sphere – this is even better! An orange sphere around you. Or a golden sphere of a good, positive, and healthy relationship around you. The golden sphere is the highest energy, it is all-inclusive! It is the most intelligent and wise and the strongest and most powerful energy. It is like the sun.

Feel that the sphere is full of energy, light, and power. Full of the energy of a good, positive, and healthy relationship. And you are inside it! You can see or feel this energy as orange energy or as white or golden. In all cases, the white or golden energy is ideal. White is the energy of life and it includes everything, all possibilities, while golden is the energy of spirit and consciousness, of the Supreme Source and it symbolizes the infinite and perfect wisdom, love, and power of the absolute.

You are in the sphere of a good, positive, and healthy relationship, within the energy of a good, positive, and healthy relationship!

Mentally, state (or use your own words):

"I am in the sphere of a good, positive, and healthy relationship, within the energy of a good, positive, and healthy relationship.
The energy of a good, positive, and healthy relationship surrounds me, it is all around me.
And the energy of a good, positive, and healthy relationship is inside me, it is everywhere inside me.
Supremely good and positive relationship with …… (name the person)!
Perfectly good and positive relationship with …… (name the person)!
Absolutely good and positive relationship with …… (name the person)!
A good, positive, and healthy relationship with …… (name the person) on all levels!"

You do not have to make a second or third circle or a second or third sphere. For the visualization, one circle or one sphere is enough. If, nonetheless, you feel guided to visualize more circles or spheres, go on and do it.

Finally, give thanks from your heart with the utmost love, joy, and gratitude! Open your eyes.

The highest, the most perfect relationship, with infinite love and unlimited joy!

BEAUTY

Take some sheets of white paper and a silver marker.

Sit comfortably and relax.

Take a few deep breaths, at a calm and slow pace. Inhale from the nose, slowly and deeply, taking your breath deep down into your belly and lower abdomen. Breathe out from the mouth, blowing the air gently, steadily, and slowly. Do these full, conscious, energetic breaths. They will release any tension, pressure, and burden and will fill you with energy, liveliness, and positivity.

Then, simply relax, and calm down your mind and body totally. Let go, let go completely.

Feel joy and have a wonderful sense of joyful anticipation, thinking about what you are going to do! You are going to give beauty to yourself, you are going to place your personal energy within greater beauty – spiritual and energetic beauty! You are about to bring forth and experience perfect beauty, total beauty, beauty on all levels!

Take the marker and one sheet of paper and write your name in the center of the paper. Your forename and then your surname under it. You can write your official, complete name or the one you use in your daily encounters. You can also use your middle name, if you have one. Simply write it under your forename and above your surname.

You can also just write the initials of your forename and surname. You can even not write down your name at all. Instead, you may write or draw something on the paper that represents/symbolizes you. For instance, you can make a dot, draw a star, or a human stick figure, as a symbol for yourself. What you have in mind – your intention – is the primary and most important element in this work and the design is secondary; it is merely symbolic.

Think that, while using the marker and drawing a circle around your name, this circle symbolizes the energy and the quality you want to bring forth and experience. The ideal state/condition you want to experience. In this case, it is Beauty.

Draw the circle around your complete name. Do it slowly, meditatively. It does not matter how large the circle is – as long as it encircles your name, that is, until it includes you. It does not have to be a perfect circle; it can be clumsy. Also, it does not matter whether you draw the circle in a left or right direction.

Do it slowly and think that what you do has great power, great power in energetic and spiritual terms.

Keep your intention in mind while you draw the circle. What does it mean? Why are you doing this?

Affirm it, either mentally or out loud:
"I create a circle of beauty around me...
A circle of beauty, around me...
I place myself within a circle of beauty...
Myself, within beauty...
I am within beauty..."

You can also repeat the quality/energy:

"Beauty... Beauty... Beauty..."

Or you can repeat both affirmations:

"Beauty... Beauty... Beauty...
I create a circle of beauty around me...
A circle of beauty around me...
I place myself within a circle of beauty...
Myself, within beauty...
I am within beauty..."

There is no right or wrong in doing this. Do it in your own way, using your own creativity, inner guidance, and intuition. You may use your own wording, affirm it in your own way. Just have a clear intention: in this case, Beauty.

Repeat and draw the circle over and over with this color, repeating the thoughts, making adjustments, and enhancing them, making the color of the circle more intense, vivid, and uniform. Each time, re-affirm your intention for beauty.

Then, pause for a while and look at the circle and think once more what it stands for, what it means. Do you feel the energy? Relax and notice. You can also take some slow, full, deep breaths.

You can enhance and empower this energy even more!

Using the same silver color, design a second larger circle around the first one. Think of what this second larger circle means:

"Greater beauty around me...
Myself, within greater beauty...
I am in greater beauty...
More beauty...
Even more beauty...
Much more beauty...
Around myself and me in the center of it..."

Keep moving the marker around, making the circle bolder and stronger. Do it in a steady, slow, and meditative manner. Keep the above statement in your mind or repeat it out loud. Once more, you can use your own words but focus on your intention for even greater beauty.

Make another pause and observe the drawing, and notice how you feel its energy. It works, it starts to manifest! It is manifesting its effects and it is powerful! You can also take some more deep, slow, full breaths.

Now let's take this to the maximum, to its greatest height and power.

Make a third, even larger circle, around the second one. Again, in the color silver. It symbolizes the highest possible level of energy, the greatest possible beauty! Absolute, perfect, total, divine beauty! Beauty on all levels!

Think about this meaning, as you draw the circle, slowly and meditatively. Repeat the circle a few times, over and over, and each time, think or say out loud the following:

"Perfect beauty around me...
Myself, in perfect beauty...
I am within perfect beauty...
The highest level of beauty!
The greatest, the supreme beauty!
Absolute and perfect beauty!
Total and complete beauty!
Beauty on all levels!"

As always, you can use your own wording, keeping in mind your intention for the highest level of this energy, the greatest possible beauty.

Stop and relax once more, noticing and observing everything. Feel the amazing energy and power! Stay for a few moments in this high positive state, receiving and experiencing all that goodness! You can also take some more deep, slow, full breaths.

For this third circle, the third level of this work, you can also use a different color, a golden one. The color gold symbolizes the golden light, the highest spiritual light. The highest level of energy and the highest level of consciousness; super-consciousness, spiritual or divine consciousness. The golden light is the light of Spirit, the Logos, and the Source/the Absolute. It is pure wisdom, pure love, and pure power... infinite wisdom – infinite love – infinite power and perfect wisdom – perfect love – perfect power!

This technique can be done using other colors too. Instead of the silver color, you may use any color you want. You could also make more circles, as many as you want. You control and define what it is that you do, what energy/quality you create, and in what way. Just be aware, know what it is that you're doing, why you are doing each move, the purpose behind each thing.

For example, you can use all the colors, symbolizing different aspects and qualities of beauty, or meaning beauty on different levels and for different areas of your life.

Try both: beauty with a variety of different colors and beauty using only the silver color, or with a combination of silver and gold at the end.

You can do just one circle. Leave the drawing as it is and then, after some time has passed or even days later, add a second circle or a third one. Once again, there is no right or wrong; you will be guided. Maybe you make many circles, then decide they are not needed, and so you do the process again, with just one circle this time. Follow your intuition.

Make the process esoterically, calmly, meditatively, and make pauses to feel the energy. Take deep breaths at the beginning and at the end of this exercise and during its practice. Focus on your purpose, clarify your intention, before you begin to design and as you design. Hold your intention. Every now and then, think of why you do what you do, what it means, what it stands for. And at the end, remain in this state, meditating for a few minutes, feeling the wonderful energy, the higher level you have entered!

STRENGTHENING THE PROCESS

There are two ways to reinforce this technique: to fill the circle with color and to add visualization.

COLOR FILLING

Fill the circle with the color silver. Color inside the circle line, slowly and calmly, filling in the white area, and covering your name. You do this so as to fill the space with energy. Your aura and your body. It's like filling your body with color, with energy, with the quality you want – in this case, Beauty!

Think about what you are doing. Have a clear intention in your mind as you fill the circle with color:

"I fill myself with beauty, with the energy of beauty.
My aura, my energy, my body, is filled with beauty, with the energy of beauty!
Beauty everywhere around me and everywhere inside me...
Beauty everywhere around me and everywhere inside me...
Beauty everywhere around me and everywhere inside me... "

Or you can use your own words.

Color and fill the whole circle.

You can also fill the space between the first and second circle and between the second and third circle as well, although this is not so important. Do it though, if you feel like it.

Since you have covered your name with color and you can no longer see it, rewrite it down below, below the circles, at the bottom of the paper.

VISUALIZATION

If you want to see more immediate results, add visualization into the process. You can do it at the beginning or at the end. Or twice, both at the beginning and at the end. This empowers the process to the highest degree!

Gently close your eyes, take some slow and deep breaths, and then let go. Relax your body and mind.

Visualize the circle of beauty around you. You can envision a silver, white, or golden circle. Or of some other color. You can also visualize a sphere – this is even better! A silver sphere of beauty around you. Or a golden sphere of beauty around you. The golden sphere is the highest energy – it is all-inclusive! It is the most intelligent and wise and the strongest and most powerful energy. It is like the sun.

Feel that the sphere is full of energy, light, and power. Full of beauty. And you are inside it! You can see or feel this energy as silver energy or as white or golden. In all cases, white or golden energy is ideal. White is the energy of life and it includes everything, all possibilities, while golden is the energy of Spirit and consciousness, of the Supreme Source and it symbolizes the infinite and perfect wisdom, love, and power of the absolute.

You are in the sphere of beauty, within the energy of beauty!

Mentally, state (or use your own words):

"I am in the sphere of beauty, within the energy of beauty.
The energy of beauty surrounds me; it is all around me.
And the energy of beauty is inside me, it is everywhere inside me.
Supreme beauty!
Perfect beauty!
Absolute beauty!
Beauty on all levels!"

You do not have to make a second or third circle or a second or third sphere. For the visualization, one circle or one sphere is enough. If, nonetheless, you feel guided to visualize more circles or spheres, go on and do it.

Finally, give thanks from your heart with the utmost love, joy, and gratitude! Open your eyes.

The highest, the most perfect beauty, with infinite love and unlimited joy!

YOUTHFULNESS

Take some sheets of white paper and a silver marker.

Sit comfortably and relax.

Take a few deep breaths, at a calm and slow pace. Inhale from the nose, slowly and deeply, taking your breath deep down into your belly and lower abdomen. Breathe out from the mouth, blowing the air gently, steadily, and slowly. Do these full, conscious, energetic breaths. They will release any tension, pressure, and burden and will fill you with energy, liveliness, and positivity.

Then, simply relax, and calm down your mind and body totally. Let go, let go completely.

Feel joy and have a wonderful sense of joyful anticipation, thinking about what you are going to do! You are going to give the energy of youthfulness to yourself, you are going to place your personal energy within greater youthfulness – spiritual and energetic youthfulness! You are about to bring forth and experience perfect youthfulness, total youthfulness, youthfulness on all levels!

Take the marker and one sheet of paper and write your name in the center of the paper. Your forename and then your sur-

name under it. You can write your official, complete name or the one you use in your daily encounters. You can also use your middle name, if you have one. Simply write it under your forename and above your surname.

You can also just write the initials of your forename and surname. You can even not write down your name at all. Instead, you may write or draw something on the paper that represents/symbolizes you. For instance, you can make a dot, draw a star, or a human stick figure, as a symbol for yourself. What you have in mind – your intention – is the primary and most important element in this work and the design is secondary; it is merely symbolic.

Think that, while using the marker and drawing a circle around your name, this circle symbolizes the energy and the quality you want to bring forth and experience. The ideal state/condition you want to experience. In this case, it is Youthfulness.

Draw the circle around your complete name. Do it slowly, meditatively. It does not matter how large the circle is – as long as it encircles your name, that is, until it includes you. It does not have to be a perfect circle; it can be clumsy. Also, it does not matter whether you draw the circle in a left or right direction.

Do it slowly and think that what you do has great power, great power in energetic and spiritual terms.

Keep your intention in mind while you draw the circle. What does it mean? Why are you doing this?
Affirm it, either mentally or out loud:

"I create a circle of youthfulness around me...
A circle of youthfulness, around me...
I place myself within a circle of youthfulness...
Myself, within youthfulness...
I am within youthfulness..."

You can also repeat the quality/energy:

"Youthfulness... Youthfulness... Youthfulness..."

Or you can repeat both affirmations:

"Youthfulness... Youthfulness... Youthfulness...
I create a circle of youthfulness around me...
A circle of youthfulness around me...
I place myself within a circle of youthfulness...
Myself, within youthfulness...
I am within youthfulness..."

There is no right or wrong in doing this. Do it in your own way, using your own creativity, inner guidance, and intuition. You may use your own wording, affirm it in your own way. Just have a clear intention: in this case, Youthfulness.

Repeat and draw the circle over and over with this color, repeating the thoughts, making adjustments, and enhancing

them, making the color of the circle more intense, vivid, and uniform. Each time, re-affirm your intention for youthfulness. Then, pause for a while and look at the circle and think once more what it stands for, what it means. Do you feel the energy? Relax and notice. You can also take some slow, full, deep breaths.

You can enhance and empower this energy even more!

Using the same silver color, design a second larger circle around the first one. Think of what this second larger circle means:

"Greater youthfulness around me...
Myself, within greater youthfulness...
I am in greater youthfulness...
More youthfulness...
Even more youthfulness...
Much more youthfulness...
Around myself and me in the center of it..."

Keep moving the marker around, making the circle bolder and stronger. Do it in a steady, slow, and meditative manner. Keep the above statement in your mind or repeat it out loud. Once more, you can use your own words but focus on your intention for even greater youthfulness.

Make another pause and observe the drawing, and notice how you feel its energy. It works, it starts to manifest! It is manifesting its effects and it is powerful! You can also take some more deep, slow, full breaths.

Now let's take this to the maximum, to its greatest height and power.

Make a third, even larger circle, around the second one. Again, in the color silver. It symbolizes the highest possible level of energy, the greatest possible youthfulness! Absolute, perfect, total, divine youthfulness! Youthfulness on all levels!

Think about this meaning, as you draw the circle, slowly and meditatively. Repeat the circle a few times, over and over, and each time, think or say out loud the following:

"Perfect youthfulness around me...
Myself, in perfect youthfulness...
I am within perfect youthfulness...
The highest level of youthfulness!
The greatest, the supreme youthfulness!
Absolute and perfect youthfulness!
Total and complete youthfulness!
Youthfulness on all levels!"

As always, you can use your own wording, keeping in mind your intention for the highest level of this energy, the greatest possible youthfulness.

Stop and relax once more, noticing and observing everything. Feel the amazing energy and power! Stay for a few moments in this high positive state, receiving and experiencing all that goodness! You can also take some more deep, slow, full breaths.

For this third circle, the third level of this work, you can also use a different color, a golden one. The color gold symbolizes the golden light, the highest spiritual light. The highest level of energy and the highest level of consciousness; super-consciousness, spiritual or divine consciousness. The golden light is the light of Spirit, the Logos, and the Source/the Absolute. It is pure wisdom, pure love, and pure power... infinite wisdom – infinite love – infinite power and perfect wisdom – perfect love – perfect power!

This technique can be done using other colors too. Instead of the silver color, you may use any color you want. You could also make more circles, as many as you want. You control and define what it is that you do, what energy/quality you create, and in what way. Just be aware, know what it is that you're doing, why you are doing each move, the purpose behind each thing.

For example, you can use all the colors, symbolizing different aspects and qualities of youthfulness, or meaning youthfulness on different levels and for different areas of your life.

Try both: youthfulness with a variety of different colors and youthfulness using only the silver color, or with a combination of silver and gold at the end.

You can do just one circle. Leave the drawing as it is and then, after some time has passed or even days later, add a second circle or a third one. Once again, there is no right or wrong; you will be guided. Maybe you make many circles, then decide they are not needed, and so you do the process again, with just one circle this time. Follow your intuition.

Make the process esoterically, calmly, meditatively, and make pauses to feel the energy. Take deep breaths at the beginning and at the end of this exercise and during its practice. Focus on your purpose, clarify your intention, before you begin to design and as you design. Hold your intention. Every now and then, think of why you do what you do, what it means, what it stands for. And at the end, remain in this state, meditating for a few minutes, feeling the wonderful energy, the higher level you have entered!

STRENGTHENING THE PROCESS

There are two ways to reinforce this technique: to fill the circle with color and to add visualization.

COLOR FILLING

Fill the circle with the color silver. Color inside the circle line, slowly and calmly, filling in the white area, and covering your name. You do this so as to fill the space with energy. Your aura and your body. It's like filling your body with color, with energy, with the quality you want – in this case, Youthfulness!

Think about what you are doing. Have a clear intention in your mind as you fill the circle with color:

"I fill myself with youthfulness, with the energy of youthfulness.
My aura, my energy, my body, is filled with youthfulness, with the energy of youthfulness!
Youthfulness everywhere around me and everywhere inside me...
Youthfulness everywhere around me and everywhere inside me...
Youthfulness everywhere around me and everywhere inside me... "

Or you can use your own words.

Color and fill the whole circle.

You can also fill the space between the first and second circle and between the second and third circle as well, although this is not so important. Do it though, if you feel like it.

Since you have covered your name with color and you can no longer see it, rewrite it down below, below the circles, at the bottom of the paper.

VISUALIZATION

If you want to see more immediate results, add visualization into the process. You can do it at the beginning or at the end. Or twice, both at the beginning and at the end. This empowers the process to the highest degree!

Gently close your eyes, take some slow and deep breaths, and then let go. Relax your body and mind.
Visualize the circle of youthfulness around you. You can envision a silver, white, or golden circle. Or of some other color. You can also visualize a sphere – this is even better! A silver sphere of youthfulness around you. Or a golden sphere of youthfulness around you. The golden sphere is the highest energy – it is all-inclusive! It is the most intelligent and wise and the strongest and most powerful energy. It is like the sun.

Feel that the sphere is full of energy, light, and power. Full of youthfulness. And you are inside it! You can see or feel this energy as silver energy or as white or golden. In all cases, white or golden energy is ideal. White is the energy of life and it includes everything, all possibilities, while golden is the energy of Spirit and consciousness, of the Supreme Source and it symbolizes the infinite and perfect wisdom, love, and power of the absolute.

You are in the sphere of youthfulness, within the energy of youthfulness!

Mentally, state (or use your own words):

"I am in the sphere of youthfulness, within the energy of youthfulness.

The energy of youthfulness surrounds me; it is all around me. And the energy of youthfulness is inside me, it is everywhere inside me.
Supreme youthfulness!
Perfect youthfulness!
Absolute youthfulness!
Youthfulness on all levels!"

You do not have to make a second or third circle or a second or third sphere. For the visualization, one circle or one sphere is enough. If, nonetheless, you feel guided to visualize more circles or spheres, go on and do it.

Finally, give thanks from your heart with the utmost love, joy, and gratitude! Open your eyes.

The highest, the most perfect youthfulness, with infinite love and unlimited joy!

IDEAL BODY WEIGHT

Take some sheets of white paper and a silver marker.

Sit comfortably and relax.

Take a few deep breaths, at a calm and slow pace. Inhale from the nose, slowly and deeply, taking your breath deep down into your belly and lower abdomen. Breathe out from the mouth, blowing the air gently, steadily, and slowly. Do these full, conscious, energetic breaths. They will release any tension, pressure, and burden and will fill you with energy, liveliness, and positivity.

Then, simply relax, and calm down your mind and body totally. Let go, let go completely.

Feel joy and have a wonderful sense of joyful anticipation, thinking about what you are going to do! You are going to give the energy of your ideal body weight to yourself, you are going to place your personal energy within the energy of your ideal body weight! You are about to bring forth and experience the perfect state of your ideal body weight, the total state of your ideal body weight, your ideal body weight on all levels!

Take the marker and one sheet of paper and write your name in the center of the paper. Your forename and then your sur-

name under it. You can write your official, complete name or the one you use in your daily encounters. You can also use your middle name, if you have one. Simply write it under your forename and above your surname.

You can also just write the initials of your forename and surname. You can even not write down your name at all. Instead, you may write or draw something on the paper that represents/symbolizes you. For instance, you can make a dot, draw a star, or a human stick figure, as a symbol for yourself. What you have in mind – your intention – is the primary and most important element in this work and the design is secondary; it is merely symbolic.

Think that, while using the marker and drawing a circle around your name, this circle symbolizes the energy and the quality you want to bring forth and experience. The ideal state/condition you want to experience. In this case, it is Your Ideal Body Weight.

Draw the circle around your complete name. Do it slowly, meditatively. It does not matter how large the circle is – as long as it encircles your name, that is, until it includes you. It does not have to be a perfect circle; it can be clumsy. Also, it does not matter whether you draw the circle in a left or right direction.

Do it slowly and think that what you do has great power, great power in energetic and spiritual terms.

Keep your intention in mind while you draw the circle. What does it mean? Why are you doing this?
Affirm it, either mentally or out loud:

"I create a circle of my ideal body weight around me...
A circle of my ideal body weight, around me...
I place myself within a circle of my ideal body weight...
Myself, within my ideal body weight...
I am within my ideal body weight..."

You can also repeat the quality/energy:

"My ideal body weight... My ideal body weight... My ideal body weight..."

Or you can repeat both affirmations:

"My ideal body weight... My ideal body weight... My ideal body weight...
I create a circle of my ideal body weight around me...
A circle of my ideal body weight around me...
I place myself within a circle of my ideal body weight...
Myself, within my ideal body weight...
I am within my ideal body weight..."

There is no right or wrong in doing this. Do it in your own way, using your own creativity, inner guidance, and intuition. You may use your own wording, affirm it in your own way. Just have a clear intention: in this case, Your Ideal Body Weight.

Repeat and draw the circle over and over with this color, repeating the thoughts, making adjustments, and enhancing them, making the color of the circle more intense, vivid, and uniform. Each time, re-affirm your intention for ideal body weight.

Then, pause for a while and look at the circle and think once more what it stands for, what it means. Do you feel the energy? Relax and notice. You can also take some slow, full, deep breaths.

You can enhance and empower this energy even more!

Using the same silver color, design a second larger circle around the first one. Think of what this second larger circle means:

"Greater energy of my ideal body weight around me...
Myself, within greater energy of my ideal body weight...
I am in greater energy of my ideal body weight...
More energy of my ideal body weight...
Even more energy of my ideal body weight...
Much more energy of my ideal body weight...
Around myself and me in the center of it..."

Keep moving the marker around, making the circle bolder and stronger. Do it in a steady, slow, and meditative manner. Keep the above statement in your mind or repeat it out loud. Once more, you can use your own words but focus on your intention for even more energy of your ideal body weight.

Make another pause and observe the drawing, and notice how you feel its energy. It works, it starts to manifest! It is manifesting its effects and it is powerful! You can also take some more deep, slow, full breaths.

Now let's take this to the maximum, to its greatest height and power.

Make a third, even larger circle, around the second one. Again, in the color silver. It symbolizes the highest possible level of energy, the greatest possible energy of your ideal body weight! Absolute, perfect, total, divine ideal body weight! Ideal body weight on all levels!

Think about this meaning, as you draw the circle, slowly and meditatively. Repeat the circle a few times, over and over, and each time, think or say out loud the following:

"The energy of my perfect ideal body weight around me...
Myself, in the energy of my perfect ideal body weight...
I am within my perfect ideal body weight...
The highest level of energy of my ideal body weight!
The greatest, the supreme energy of my ideal body weight!
Absolutely perfect ideal body weight!
Totally perfect ideal body weight!
Perfect and ideal body weight on all levels!"

As always, you can use your own wording, keeping in mind your intention for the highest level of this energy, the greatest possible energy of your ideal body weight.

Stop and relax once more, noticing and observing everything. Feel the amazing energy and power! Stay for a few moments in this high positive state, receiving and experiencing all that goodness! You can also take some more deep, slow, full breaths.

For this third circle, the third level of this work, you can also use a different color, a golden one. The color gold symbolizes the golden light, the highest spiritual light. The highest level of energy and the highest level of consciousness; super-consciousness, spiritual or divine consciousness. The golden light is the light of Spirit, the Logos, and the Source/the Absolute. It is pure wisdom, pure love, and pure power... infinite wisdom – infinite love – infinite power and perfect wisdom – perfect love – perfect power!

This technique can be done using other colors too. Instead of the silver color, you may use any color you want. You could also make more circles, as many as you want. You control and define what it is that you do, what energy/quality you create, and in what way. Just be aware, know what it is that you're doing, why you are doing each move, the purpose behind each thing.

For example, you can use all the colors, symbolizing different aspects and qualities of your ideal body weight, or meaning your ideal body weight on different levels.

Try both: your ideal body weight with a variety of different colors and your ideal body weight using only the silver color, or with a combination of silver and gold at the end.

You can do just one circle. Leave the drawing as it is and then, after some time has passed or even days later, add a second circle or a third one. Once again, there is no right or wrong; you will be guided. Maybe you make many circles, then decide they are not needed, and so you do the process again, with just one circle this time. Follow your intuition.

Make the process esoterically, calmly, meditatively, and make pauses to feel the energy. Take deep breaths at the beginning and at the end of this exercise and during its practice. Focus on your purpose, clarify your intention, before you begin to design and as you design. Hold your intention. Every now and then, think of why you do what you do, what it means, what it stands for. And at the end, remain in this state, meditating for a few minutes, feeling the wonderful energy, the higher level you have entered!

STRENGTHENING THE PROCESS

There are two ways to reinforce this technique: to fill the circle with color and to add visualization.

COLOR FILLING

Fill the circle with the color silver. Color inside the circle line, slowly and calmly, filling in the white area, and covering your name. You do this so as to fill the space with energy. Your aura and your body. It's like filling your body with color, with energy, with the quality you want – in this case, Ideal Body Weight!

Think about what you are doing. Have a clear intention in your mind as you fill the circle with color:

"I fill myself with the energy of my ideal body weight.
My aura, my energy, my body, is filled with the energy of my ideal body weight!
My ideal body weight everywhere around me and everywhere inside me...
My ideal body weight everywhere around me and everywhere inside me...
My ideal body weight everywhere around me and everywhere inside me... "

Or you can use your own words.

Color and fill the whole circle.

You can also fill the space between the first and second circle and between the second and third circle as well, although this is not so important. Do it though, if you feel like it.

Since you have covered your name with color and you can no longer see it, rewrite it down below, below the circles, at the bottom of the paper.

VISUALIZATION

If you want to see more immediate results, add visualization into the process. You can do it at the beginning or at the end. Or twice, both at the beginning and at the end. This empowers the process to the highest degree!

ENERGY CIRCLES

Gently close your eyes, take some slow and deep breaths, and then let go. Relax your body and mind.

Visualize the circle of the energy of your ideal body weight around you. You can envision a silver, white, or golden circle. Or of some other color. You can also visualize a sphere – this is even better! A silver sphere of the energy of your ideal body weight around you. Or a golden sphere of the energy of your ideal body weight around you. The golden sphere is the highest energy – it is all-inclusive! It is the most intelligent and wise and the strongest and most powerful energy. It is like the sun.

Feel that the sphere is full of energy, light, and power. Full of the energy of your ideal body weight. And you are inside it! You can see or feel this energy as silver energy or as white or golden. In all cases, white or golden energy is ideal. White is the energy of life and it includes everything, all possibilities, while golden is the energy of Spirit and consciousness, of the Supreme Source and it symbolizes the infinite and perfect wisdom, love, and power of the absolute.

You are in the sphere of your ideal body weight, within the energy of your ideal body weight!

Mentally, state (or use your own words):

"I am in the sphere of my ideal body weight, within the energy of my ideal body weight.
The energy of my ideal body weight surrounds me; it is all around me.

And the energy of my ideal body weight is inside me, it is everywhere inside me.
Supremely ideal body weight!
Perfectly ideal body weight!
Absolutely ideal body weight!
Ideal body weight on all levels!"

You do not have to make a second or third circle or a second or third sphere. For the visualization, one circle or one sphere is enough. If, nonetheless, you feel guided to visualize more circles or spheres, go on and do it.

Finally, give thanks from your heart with the utmost love, joy, and gratitude! Open your eyes.

The most perfect ideal body weight, with infinite love and unlimited joy!

ENERGETIC CLEARING AND PURIFICATION

Take some sheets of white paper and a red marker.

Sit comfortably and relax.

Take a few deep breaths, at a calm and slow pace. Inhale from the nose, slowly and deeply, taking your breath deep down into your belly and lower abdomen. Breathe out from the mouth, blowing the air gently, steadily, and slowly. Do these full, conscious, energetic breaths. They will release any tension, pressure, and burden and will fill you with energy, liveliness, and positivity.

Then, simply relax, and calm down your mind and body totally. Let go, let go completely.

Feel joy and have a wonderful sense of joyful anticipation, thinking about what you are going to do! You are going to give an energetic clearing and purification to yourself, you are going to place your personal energy within greater energetic clearing and purification! You are about to bring forth and experience a perfect energetic clearing and purification, a total energetic clearing and purification, an energetic clearing and purification on all levels!

Take the marker and one sheet of paper and write your name in the center of the paper. Your forename and then your surname under it. You can write your official, complete name or the one you use in your daily encounters. You can also use your middle name, if you have one. Simply write it under your forename and above your surname.

You can also just write the initials of your forename and surname. You can even not write down your name at all. Instead, you may write or draw something on the paper that represents/symbolizes you. For instance, you can make a dot, draw a star, or a human stick figure, as a symbol for yourself. What you have in mind – your intention – is the primary and most important element in this work and the design is secondary; it is merely symbolic.

Think that, while using the marker and drawing a circle around your name, this circle symbolizes the energy and the quality you want to bring forth and experience. The ideal state/condition you want to experience. In this case, it is Energetic Clearing and Purification.

Draw the circle around your complete name. Do it slowly, meditatively. It does not matter how large the circle is – as long as it encircles your name, that is, until it includes you. It does not have to be a perfect circle; it can be clumsy. Also, it does not matter whether you draw the circle in a left or right direction.

Do it slowly and think that what you do has great power, great power in energetic and spiritual terms.

Keep your intention in mind while you draw the circle. What does it mean? Why are you doing this?

Affirm it, either mentally or out loud:

"I create a circle of energetic clearing and purification around me...
A circle of energetic clearing and purification, around me...
I place myself within a circle of energetic clearing and purification...
Myself, within energetic clearing and purification...
I am within energetic clearing and purification..."

You can also repeat the quality/energy:

"Energetic clearing and purification... Energetic clearing and purification... Energetic clearing and purification..."

Or you can repeat both affirmations:

"Energetic clearing and purification... Energetic clearing and purification... Energetic clearing and purification...
I create a circle of energetic clearing and purification around me...
A circle of energetic clearing and purification around me...
I place myself within a circle of energetic clearing and purification...
Myself, within energetic clearing and purification...
I am within energetic clearing and purification..."

There is no right or wrong in doing this. Do it in your own way, using your own creativity, inner guidance, and intuition. You may use your own wording, affirm it in your own way. Just have a clear intention: in this case, Energetic Clearing and Purification.

Repeat and draw the circle over and over with this color, repeating the thoughts, making adjustments, and enhancing them, making the color of the circle more intense, vivid, and uniform. Each time, re-affirm your intention for energetic clearing and purification.

Then, pause for a while and look at the circle and think once more what it stands for, what it means. Do you feel the energy? Relax and notice. You can also take some slow, full, deep breaths.

You can enhance and empower this energy even more!

Using the same red color, design a second larger circle around the first one. Think of what this second larger circle means:

"Greater energetic clearing and purification around me...
Myself, within greater energetic clearing and purification...
I am in greater energetic clearing and purification...
More energetic clearing and purification...
Even more energetic clearing and purification...
Much more energetic clearing and purification...
Around myself and me in the center of it..."

Keep moving the marker around, making the circle bolder and stronger. Do it in a steady, slow, and meditative manner. Keep the above statement in your mind or repeat it out loud. Once more, you can use your own words but focus on your intention for even greater energetic clearing and purification.

Make another pause and observe the drawing, and notice how you feel its energy. It works, it starts to manifest! It is manifesting its effects and it is powerful! You can also take some more deep, slow, full breaths.

Now let's take this to the maximum, to its greatest height and power.

Make a third, even larger circle, around the second one. Again, in the color red. It symbolizes the highest possible level of energy, the greatest possible energetic clearing and purification! Absolute, perfect, total, divine energetic clearing and purification! Energetic clearing and purification on all levels!

Think about this meaning, as you draw the circle, slowly and meditatively. Repeat the circle a few times, over and over, and each time, think or say out loud the following:

"Perfect energetic clearing and purification around me...
Myself, in perfect energetic clearing and purification...
I am within perfect energetic clearing and purification...
The highest level of energetic clearing and purification!

The greatest, the supreme energetic clearing and purification!
Absolute and perfect energetic clearing and purification!
Total and complete energetic clearing and purification!
Energetic clearing and purification on all levels!"
As always, you can use your own wording, keeping in mind your intention for the highest level of this energy, the greatest possible energetic clearing and purification.

Stop and relax once more, noticing and observing everything. Feel the amazing energy and power! Stay for a few moments in this high positive state, receiving and experiencing all that goodness! You can also take some more deep, slow, full breaths.

For this third circle, the third level of this work, you can also use a different color, a golden one. The color gold symbolizes the golden light, the highest spiritual light. The highest level of energy and the highest level of consciousness; super-consciousness, spiritual or divine consciousness. The golden light is the light of Spirit, the Logos, and the Source/the Absolute. It is pure wisdom, pure love, and pure power... infinite wisdom – infinite love – infinite power and perfect wisdom – perfect love – perfect power!

This technique can be done using other colors too. Instead of the red color, you may use any color you want. You could also make more circles, as many as you want. You control and define what it is that you do, what energy/quality you create, and in what way. Just be aware, know what it is that you're doing, why you are doing each move, the purpose behind each thing.

For example, you can use all the colors, symbolizing different aspects and qualities of energetic clearing and purification, or meaning energetic clearing and purification on different levels and for different areas of your life.

Try both: energetic clearing and purification with a variety of different colors and energetic clearing and purification using only the red color, or with a combination of red and gold at the end.

You can do just one circle. Leave the drawing as it is and then, after some time has passed or even days later, add a second circle or a third one. Once again, there is no right or wrong; you will be guided. Maybe you make many circles, then decide they are not needed, and so you do the process again, with just one circle this time. Follow your intuition.

Make the process esoterically, calmly, meditatively, and make pauses to feel the energy. Take deep breaths at the beginning and at the end of this exercise and during its practice. Focus on your purpose, clarify your intention, before you begin to design and as you design. Hold your intention. Every now and then, think of why you do what you do, what it means, what it stands for. And at the end, remain in this state, meditating for a few minutes, feeling the wonderful energy, the higher level you have entered!

STRENGTHENING THE PROCESS

There are two ways to reinforce this technique: to fill the circle with color and to add visualization.

COLOR FILLING

Fill the circle with the color red. Color inside the circle line, slowly and calmly, filling in the white area, and covering your name. You do this so as to fill the space with energy. Your aura and your body. It's like filling your body with color, with energy, with the quality you want – in this case, Energetic Clearing and Purification!

Think about what you are doing. Have a clear intention in your mind as you fill the circle with color:

"I fill myself with energetic clearing and purification, with the energy of energetic clearing and purification.
My aura, my energy, my body, is filled with energetic clearing and purification, with the energy of energetic clearing and purification!
Energetic clearing and purification everywhere around me and everywhere inside me...
Energetic clearing and purification everywhere around me and everywhere inside me...
Energetic clearing and purification everywhere around me and everywhere inside me... "

Or you can use your own words.

Color and fill the whole circle.

You can also fill the space between the first and second circle and between the second and third circle as well, although this is not so important. Do it though, if you feel like it.

Since you have covered your name with color and you can no longer see it, rewrite it down below, below the circles, at the bottom of the paper.

VISUALIZATION

If you want to see more immediate results, add visualization into the process. You can do it at the beginning or at the end. Or twice, both at the beginning and at the end. This empowers the process to the highest degree!

Gently close your eyes, take some slow and deep breaths, and then let go. Relax your body and mind.

Visualize the circle of energetic clearing and purification around you. You can envision a red, white, or golden circle. Or of some other color. You can also visualize a sphere – this is even better! A red sphere of energetic clearing and purification around you. Or a golden sphere of energetic clearing and purification around you. The golden sphere is the highest energy – it is all-inclusive! It is the most intelligent and wise and the strongest and most powerful energy. It is like the sun.

Feel that the sphere is full of energy, light, and power. Full of energetic clearing and purification. And you are inside it! You can see or feel this energy as red energy or as white or golden. In all cases, white or golden energy is ideal. White is the energy of life and it includes everything, all possibilities, while golden is the energy of Spirit and consciousness, of the Supreme Source and it symbolizes the infinite and perfect wisdom, love, and power of the absolute.

You are in the sphere of energetic clearing and purification, within the energy of energetic clearing and purification!

Mentally, state (or use your own words):

"I am in the sphere of energetic clearing and purification, within the energy of energetic clearing and purification.
The energy of energetic clearing and purification surrounds me; it is all around me.
And the energy of energetic clearing and purification is inside me, it is everywhere inside me.
Supreme energetic clearing and purification!
Perfect energetic clearing and purification!
Absolute energetic clearing and purification!
Energetic clearing and purification on all levels!"

You do not have to make a second or third circle or a second or third sphere. For the visualization, one circle or one sphere is enough. If, nonetheless, you feel guided to visualize more circles or spheres, go on and do it.

Finally, give thanks from your heart with the utmost love, joy, and gratitude! Open your eyes.

The highest, the most perfect energetic clearing and purification, with infinite love and unlimited joy!

DETOXIFICATION AND RELEASE OF UNHEALTHY HABITS AND ADDICTIONS

Take some sheets of white paper and a red marker.

Sit comfortably and relax.

Take a few deep breaths, at a calm and slow pace. Inhale from the nose, slowly and deeply, taking your breath deep down into your belly and lower abdomen. Breathe out from the mouth, blowing the air gently, steadily, and slowly. Do these full, conscious, energetic breaths. They will release any tension, pressure, and burden and will fill you with energy, liveliness, and positivity.

Then, simply relax, and calm down your mind and body totally. Let go, let go completely.

Feel joy and have a wonderful sense of joyful anticipation, thinking about what you are going to do! You are going to give a detoxification to yourself and a release of unhealthy habits and addictions; you are going to place your personal energy within greater detoxification and release of unhealthy habits and addictions – spiritual and energetic detoxification and release! You are about to bring forth and experience perfect detoxification and release of unhealthy habits and addictions, total detoxification and release of unhealthy habits and addictions, detoxification and release of unhealthy habits and addictions on all levels!

Take the marker and one sheet of paper and write your name in the center of the paper. Your forename and then your surname under it. You can write your official, complete name or the one you use in your daily encounters. You can also use your middle name, if you have one. Simply write it under your forename and above your surname.

You can also just write the initials of your forename and surname. You can even not write down your name at all. Instead, you may write or draw something on the paper that represents/symbolizes you. For instance, you can make a dot, draw a star, or a human stick figure, as a symbol for yourself. What you have in mind – your intention – is the primary and most important element in this work and the design is secondary; it is merely symbolic.

Think that, while using the marker and drawing draw a circle around your name, that this circle symbolizes the energy and the quality you want to bring forth and experience. The ideal state/condition you want to experience. In this case, it is Detoxification and Release of Unhealthy Habits and Addictions.

Draw the circle around your complete name and surname. Do it slowly, meditatively. It does not matter how large the circle is – as long as it encircles your name, that is, until it includes you. It does not have to be a perfect circle, it can be clumsy. Also, it does not matter whether you draw the circle in a left or right direction.

Do it slowly and think that what you do has great power, great power in energetic and spiritual terms.

Keep your intention in mind while you draw the circle. What does it mean? Why are you doing this?

Affirm it, either mentally or out loud:

"I create a circle of detoxification and release of unhealthy habits and addictions around me...
A circle of detoxification and release of unhealthy habits and addictions around me...
I place myself within a circle of detoxification and release of unhealthy habits and addictions...
Myself, within detoxification and release of unhealthy habits and addictions...
I am within detoxification and release of unhealthy habits and addictions..."

You can also repeat the quality/energy:

"Detoxification and release of unhealthy habits and addictions... Detoxification and release of unhealthy habits and addictions... Detoxification and release of unhealthy habits and addictions..."

Or you can repeat both affirmations:

"Detoxification and release of unhealthy habits and addictions... Detoxification and release of unhealthy habits and addictions... Detoxification and release of unhealthy habits and addictions...

I create a circle of detoxification and release of unhealthy habits and addictions around me...
A circle of detoxification and release of unhealthy habits and addictions around me...
I place myself within a circle of detoxification and release of unhealthy habits and addictions...
Myself, within detoxification and release of unhealthy habits and addictions...
I am within detoxification and release of unhealthy habits and addictions..."

There is no right or wrong in doing this. Do it in your own way, using your own creativity, inner guidance, and intuition. You may use your own wording, affirm it in your own way. Just have a clear intention: in this case, Detoxification and Release of Unhealthy Habits and Addictions.

Repeat and draw the circle over and over with this color, repeating the thoughts, making adjustments, and enhancing them, making the color of the circle more intense, vivid, and uniform. Each time, re-affirm your intention for detoxification and release of unhealthy habits and addictions.

Then, pause for a while and look at the circle and think once more what it stands for, what it means. Do you feel the energy? Relax and notice. You can also take some slow, full, deep breaths.

You can enhance and empower this energy even more!
Using the same red color, design a second larger circle around the first one. Think of what this second larger circle means:
"Greater detoxification and release of unhealthy habits and addictions around me...
Myself, within greater detoxification and release of unhealthy habits and addictions...
I am in greater detoxification and release of unhealthy habits and addictions...
More detoxification and release of unhealthy habits and addictions...
Even more detoxification and release of unhealthy habits and addictions...
Much more detoxification and release of unhealthy habits and addictions...
Around myself and me in the center of it..."

Keep moving the marker around, making the circle bolder and stronger. Do it in a steady, slow, and meditative manner. Keep the above statement in your mind or repeat it out loud. Once more, you can use your own words but focus on your intention for even greater detoxification and release of unhealthy habits and addictions.

Make another pause and observe the drawing, and notice how you feel its energy. It works, it starts to manifest! It is manifesting its effects and it is powerful! You can also take some more deep, slow, full breaths.

Now let's take this to the maximum, to its greatest height and power.

Make a third, even larger circle, around the second one. Again, in the color red. It symbolizes the highest possible level of energy, the greatest possible detoxification and release of unhealthy habits and addictions! Absolute, perfect, total, divine detoxification and release of unhealthy habits and addictions! Detoxification and release of unhealthy habits and addictions on all levels!

Think about this meaning, as you draw the circle, slowly and meditatively. Repeat the circle a few times, over and over, and each time, think or say out loud the following:

"Perfect detoxification and release of unhealthy habits and addictions around me...
Myself, in perfect detoxification and release of unhealthy habits and addictions...
I am within perfect detoxification and release of unhealthy habits and addictions...
The highest level of detoxification and release of unhealthy habits and addictions!
The greatest, the supreme detoxification and release of unhealthy habits and addictions!
Absolute and perfect detoxification and release of unhealthy habits and addictions!
Total and complete detoxification and release of unhealthy habits and addictions!
Detoxification and release of unhealthy habits and addictions on all levels!"

As always, you can use your own wording, keeping in mind

your intention for the highest level of this energy, the greatest possible detoxification and release of unhealthy habits and addictions.

Stop and relax once more, noticing and observing everything. Feel the amazing energy and power! Stay for a few moments in this high positive state, receiving and experiencing all that goodness! You can also take some more deep, slow, full breaths.

For this third circle, the third level of this work, you can also use a different color, a golden one. The color gold symbolizes the golden light, the highest spiritual light. The highest level of energy and the highest level of consciousness; super-consciousness, spiritual or divine consciousness. The golden light is the light of Spirit, the Logos, and the Source/the Absolute. It is pure wisdom, pure love, and pure power... infinite wisdom – infinite love – infinite power and perfect wisdom – perfect love – perfect power!

This technique can be done using other colors too. Instead of the red color, you may use any color you want. You could also make more circles, as many as you want. You control and define what it is that you do, what energy/quality you create, and in what way. Just be aware, know what it is that you're doing, why you are doing each move, the purpose behind each thing.

For example, you can use all the colors, symbolizing different aspects and qualities of detoxification and release of unhealthy habits and addictions or meaning detoxification and release of unhealthy habits and addictions on different levels and for different areas of your life.

Try both; detoxification and release of unhealthy habits and addictions with a variety of different colors and detoxification and release of unhealthy habits and addictions using only the red color or with a combination of red and gold at the end.

You can do just one circle. Leave the drawing as it is and then, after some time has passed or even days later, add a second circle or a third one. Once again, there is no right or wrong; you will be guided. Maybe you make many circles, then decide they are not needed, and so you do the process again, with just one circle this time. Follow your intuition.

Make the process esoterically, calmly, meditatively, and make pauses to feel the energy. Take deep breaths at the beginning and at the end of this exercise and during its practice. Focus on your purpose, clarify your intention, before you begin to design and as you design. Hold your intention. Every now and then, think of why you do what you do, what it means, what it stands for. And at the end, remain in this state, meditating for a few minutes, feeling the wonderful energy, the higher level you have entered!

STRENGTHENING THE PROCESS

There are two ways to reinforce this technique: to fill the circle with color and to add visualization.

COLOR FILLING

Fill the circle with the color red. Color inside the circle line, slowly and calmly, filling in the white area, and covering your name. You do this so as to fill the space with energy. Your aura and your body. It's like filling your body with color, with energy, with the quality you want – in this case, Detoxification and Release of Unhealthy Habits and Addictions!

Think about what you are doing. Have a clear intention in your mind as you fill the circle with color:

"I fill myself with detoxification and release of unhealthy habits and addictions, with the energy of detoxification and release of unhealthy habits and addictions.
My aura, my energy, my body, is filled with detoxification and release of unhealthy habits and addictions, with the energy of detoxification and release of unhealthy habits and addictions!
Detoxification and release of unhealthy habits and addictions everywhere around me and everywhere inside me...
Detoxification and release of unhealthy habits and addictions everywhere around me and everywhere inside me...
Detoxification and release of unhealthy habits and addictions everywhere around me and everywhere inside me... "

Or you can use your own words.

Color and fill the whole circle.

You can also fill the space between the first and second circle and between the second and third circle as well, although this is not so important. Do it though, if you feel like it.

Since you have covered your name with color and you can no longer see it, rewrite it down below, below the circles, at the bottom of the paper.

VISUALIZATION

If you want to see more immediate results, add visualization into the process. You can do it at the beginning or at the end. Or twice, both at the beginning and at the end. This empowers the process to the highest degree!

Gently close your eyes, take some slow and deep breaths, and then let go. Relax your body and mind.

Visualize the circle of detoxification and release of unhealthy habits and addictions around you. You can envision a red, white, or golden circle. Or of some other color. You can also visualize a sphere – this is even better! A red sphere of detoxification and release of unhealthy habits and addictions around you. Or a golden sphere of detoxification and release of unhealthy habits and addictions around you. The golden sphere is the highest energy, it is all-inclusive! It is the most intelligent and wise and the strongest and most powerful energy. It is like the sun.

Feel that the sphere is full of energy, light, and power. Full of detoxification and release of unhealthy habits and addictions.

And you are inside it! You can see or feel this energy as red energy or as white or golden. In all cases, the white or golden energy is ideal. White is the energy of life and it includes everything, all possibilities, while golden is the energy of spirit and consciousness, of the Supreme Source, and it symbolizes the infinite and perfect wisdom, love, and power of the absolute.

You are in the sphere of detoxification and release of unhealthy habits and addictions, within the energy of detoxification and release of unhealthy habits and addictions!

Mentally, state (or use your own words):

"I am in the sphere of detoxification and release of unhealthy habits and addictions, within the energy of detoxification and release of unhealthy habits and addictions.
The energy of detoxification and release of unhealthy habits and addictions surrounds me, it is all around me.
And the energy of detoxification and release of unhealthy habits and addictions is inside me, it is everywhere inside me.
Supreme detoxification and release of unhealthy habits and addictions!
Perfect detoxification and release of unhealthy habits and addictions!
Absolute detoxification and release of unhealthy habits and addictions!
Detoxification and release of unhealthy habits and addictions on all levels!"

You do not have to make a second or third circle or a second or third sphere. For the visualization, one circle or one sphere is enough. If, nonetheless, you feel guided to visualize more circles or spheres, go on and do it.

Finally, give thanks from your heart with the utmost love, joy, and gratitude! Open your eyes.

The highest, the most perfect detoxification and release of unhealthy habits and addictions, with infinite love and unlimited joy!

RELEASE OF FEAR (OR BITTERNESS, ANGER, GUILT, SADNESS OR WORRY)

For this exercise, choose the emotion you want to release from your life. You can choose fear, anger, sadness, bitterness, jealousy, guilt, tension, stress, anxiety, worry or any other negative emotion or feeling. Substitute the word fear with the emotion you want to release. Work with only one word/emotion per time.

Take some sheets of white paper and a blue marker.

Sit comfortably and relax.

Take a few deep breaths, at a calm and slow pace. Inhale from the nose, slowly and deeply, taking your breath deep down into your belly and lower abdomen. Breathe out from the mouth, blowing the air gently, steadily, and slowly. Do these full, conscious, energetic breaths. They will release any tension, pressure, and burden and will fill you with energy, liveliness, and positivity.

Then, simply relax, and calm down your mind and body totally. Let go, let go completely.

Feel joy and have a wonderful sense of joyful anticipation, thinking about what you are going to do! You are going to release fear (or any other negative feeling or emotion you have chosen) from yourself, you are going to place your personal energy within the release of fear – spiritual and energetic release of fear! You are about to bring forth and experience perfect release of fear, total release of fear, release of fear on all levels!

Take the marker and one sheet of paper and write your name in the center of the paper. Your forename and then your surname under it. You can write your official, complete name or the one you use in your daily encounters. You can also use your middle name, if you have one. Simply write it under your forename and above your surname.

You can also just write the initials of your forename and surname. You can even not write down your name at all. Instead, you may write or draw something on the paper that represents/symbolizes you. For instance, you can make a dot, draw a star, or a human stick figure, as a symbol for yourself. What you have in mind – your intention – is the primary and most important element in this work and the design is secondary; it is merely symbolic.

Think that, while using the marker and drawing a circle around your name, this circle symbolizes the energy and the quality you want to bring forth and experience. The ideal state/condition you want to experience. In this case, it is Release of Fear.

Draw the circle around your complete name and surname. Do it slowly, meditatively. It does not matter how large the circle is – as long as it encircles your name, that is, until it includes you. It does not have to be a perfect circle, it can be clumsy. Also, it does not matter whether you draw the circle in a left or right direction.

Do it slowly and think that what you do has great power, great power in energetic and spiritual terms.

Keep your intention in mind while you draw the circle. What does it mean? Why are you doing this?

Affirm it, either mentally or out loud:

"I create a circle of release of fear around me...
A circle of release of fear, around me...
I place myself within a circle of release of fear...
Myself, within release of fear...
I am within release of fear..."

You can also repeat the quality/energy:

"Release of fear... Release of fear... Release of fear..."

Or you can repeat both affirmations:

"Release of fear... Release of fear... Release of fear...
I create a circle of release of fear around me...
A circle of release of fear around me...

I place myself within a circle of release of fear...
Myself, within release of fear...
I am within release of fear..."
There is no right or wrong in doing this. Do it in your own way, using your own creativity, inner guidance, and intuition. You may use your own wording, affirm it in your own way. Just have a clear intention: in this case, Release of Fear.

Repeat and draw the circle over and over with this color, repeating the thoughts, making adjustments, and enhancing them, making the color of the circle more intense, vivid, and uniform. Each time, re-affirm your intention for release of fear.

Then, pause for a while and look at the circle and think once more what it stands for, what it means. Do you feel the energy? Relax and notice. You can also take some slow, full, deep breaths.

You can enhance and empower this energy even more!

Using the same blue color, design a second larger circle around the first one. Think of what this second larger circle means:

"Greater release of fear around me...
Myself, within greater release of fear...
I am in greater release of fear...
More release of fear...

Even more release of fear...
Much more release of fear...
Around myself and me in the center of it..."

Keep moving the marker around, making the circle bolder and stronger. Do it in a steady, slow, and meditative manner. Keep the above statement in your mind or repeat it out loud. Once more, you can use your own words but focus on your intention for even greater release of fear.

Make another pause and observe the drawing, and notice how you feel its energy. It works, it starts to manifest! It is manifesting its effects and it is powerful! You can also take some more deep, slow, full breaths.

Now let's take this to the maximum, to its greatest height and power.

Make a third, even larger circle, around the second one. Again, in the color blue. It symbolizes the highest possible level of energy, the greatest possible release of fear! Absolute, perfect, total, divine release of fear! Release of fear on all levels!

Think about this meaning, as you draw the circle, slowly and meditatively. Repeat the circle a few times, over and over, and each time, think or say out loud the following:

"Perfect release of fear around me...
Myself, in perfect release of fear...
I am within perfect release of fear...

The highest level of release of fear!
The greatest, the supreme release of fear!
Absolute and perfect release of fear!
Total and complete release of fear!
Release of fear on all levels!"

As always, you can use your own wording, keeping in mind your intention for the highest level of this energy, the greatest possible release of fear.

Stop and relax once more, noticing and observing everything. Feel the amazing energy and power! Stay for a few moments in this high positive state, receiving and experiencing all that goodness! You can also take some more deep, slow, full breaths.

For this third circle, the third level of this work, you can also use a different color, a golden one. The color gold symbolizes the golden light, the highest spiritual light. The highest level of energy and the highest level of consciousness; super-consciousness, spiritual or divine consciousness. The golden light is the light of Spirit, the Logos, and the Source/the Absolute. It is pure wisdom, pure love, and pure power... Infinite wisdom – infinite love – infinite power and perfect wisdom – perfect love – perfect power!

This technique can be done using other colors too. Instead of the blue color, you may use any color you want. You could also make more circles, as many as you want. You control and define what it is that you do, what energy/quality you create, and in what way. Just be aware, know what it is that you're doing, why you are doing each move, the purpose behind each thing. For example, you can use all the colors, symbolizing different aspects and qualities of release of fear or meaning release of fear on different levels and for different areas of your life.

Try both; release of fear with a variety of different colors and release of fear using only the blue color or with a combination of blue and gold at the end.

You can do just one circle. Leave the drawing as it is and then, after some time has passed or even days later, add a second circle or a third one. Once again, there is no right or wrong; you will be guided. Maybe you make many circles, then decide they are not needed, and so you do the process again, with just one circle this time. Follow your intuition.

Make the process esoterically, calmly, meditatively, and make pauses to feel the energy. Take deep breaths at the beginning and at the end of this exercise and during its practice. Focus on your purpose and clarify your intention, before you begin to design and as you design. Hold your intention. Every now and then, think of why you do what you do, what it means, what it stands for. And at the end, remain in this state, meditating for a few minutes, feeling the wonderful energy, the higher level you have entered!

STRENGTHENING THE PROCESS

There are two ways to reinforce this technique: to fill the circle with color and to add visualization.

COLOR FILLING

Fill the circle with the color blue. Color inside the circle line, slowly and calmly, filling in the white area, and covering your name. You do this so as to fill the space with energy. Your aura and your body. It's like filling your body with color, with energy; with the quality you want – in this case, Release of Fear!

Think about what you are doing. Have a clear intention in your mind as you fill the circle with color:

"I fill myself with the energy of release of fear.
My aura, my energy, my body, is filled with the energy of release of fear!
Release of fear everywhere around me and everywhere inside me...
Release of fear everywhere around me and everywhere inside me...
Release of fear everywhere around me and everywhere inside me..."

Or you can use your own words.

Color and fill the whole circle.

You can also fill the space between the first and second circle and between the second and third circle as well, although this is not so important. Do it though, if you feel like it.

Since you have covered your name with color and you can no

longer see it, rewrite it down below, below the circles, at the bottom of the paper.

VISUALIZATION

If you want to see more immediate results, add visualization into the process. You can do it at the beginning or at the end. Or twice, both at the beginning and at the end. This empowers the process to the highest degree!

Gently close your eyes, take some slow and deep breaths, and then let go. Relax your body and mind.

Visualize the circle of release of fear around you. You can envision a blue, white, or golden circle. Or of some other color. You can also visualize a sphere – this is even better! A blue sphere around you. Or a golden sphere of release of fear around you. The golden sphere is the highest energy; it is all-inclusive! It is the most intelligent and wise and the strongest and most powerful energy. It is like the sun.

Feel that the sphere is full of energy, light, and power. Full of the energy of release of fear. And you are inside it! You can see or feel this energy as blue energy or as white or golden. In all cases, the white or golden energy is ideal. White is the energy of life and it includes everything, all possibilities, while golden is the energy of spirit and consciousness, of the Supreme Source and it symbolizes the infinite and perfect wisdom, love, and power of the absolute.

You are in the sphere of release of fear, within the energy of release of fear!

Mentally, state (or use your own words):
"I am in the sphere of release of fear, within the energy of release of fear.
The energy of release of fear surrounds me, it is all around me.
And the energy of release of fear is inside me, it is everywhere inside me.
Supreme release of fear!
Perfect release of fear!
Absolute release of fear!
Release of fear on all levels!"

You do not have to make a second or third circle or a second or third sphere. For the visualization, one circle or one sphere is enough. If, nonetheless, you feel guided to visualize more circles or spheres, go on and do it.

Finally, give thanks from your heart with the utmost love, joy, and gratitude! Open your eyes.

The highest, the most perfect release of fear, with infinite love and unlimited joy!

EMOTIONAL HEALING

Take some sheets of white paper and a blue marker.

Sit comfortably and relax.

Take a few deep breaths, at a calm and slow pace. Inhale from the nose, slowly and deeply, taking your breath deep down into your belly and lower abdomen. Breathe out from the mouth, blowing the air gently, steadily, and slowly. Do these full, conscious, energetic breaths. They will release any tension, pressure, and burden and will fill you with energy, liveliness, and positivity.

Then, simply relax, and calm down your mind and body totally. Let go, let go completely.

Feel joy and have a wonderful sense of joyful anticipation, thinking about what you are going to do! You are going to give emotional healing to yourself, you are going to place your personal energy within greater emotional healing – spiritual and energetic emotional healing! You are about to bring forth and experience perfect emotional healing, total emotional healing, emotional healing on all levels!

Take the marker and one sheet of paper and write your name in the center of the paper. Your forename and then your sur-

name under it. You can write your official, complete name or the one you use in your daily encounters. You can also use your middle name, if you have one. Simply write it under your forename and above your surname.

You can also just write the initials of your forename and surname. You can even not write down your name at all. Instead, you may write or draw something on the paper that represents/symbolizes you. For instance, you can make a dot, draw a star, or a human stick figure, as a symbol for yourself. What you have in mind – your intention – is the primary and most important element in this work and the design is secondary; it is merely symbolic.

Think that, while using the marker and drawing a circle around your name, this circle symbolizes the energy and the quality you want to bring forth and experience. The ideal state/condition you want to experience. In this case, it is Emotional Healing.

Draw the circle around your complete name. Do it slowly, meditatively. It does not matter how large the circle is – as long as it encircles your name, that is, until it includes you. It does not have to be a perfect circle; it can be clumsy. Also, it does not matter whether you draw the circle in a left or right direction.

Do it slowly and think that what you do has great power, great power in energetic and spiritual terms.

Keep your intention in mind while you draw the circle. What does it mean? Why are you doing this?
Affirm it, either mentally or out loud:

"I create a circle of emotional healing around me...
A circle of emotional healing, around me...
I place myself within a circle of emotional healing...
Myself, within emotional healing...
I am within emotional healing..."

You can also repeat the quality/energy:

"Emotional healing... Emotional healing... Emotional healing..."

Or you can repeat both affirmations:

"Emotional healing... Emotional healing... Emotional healing...
I create a circle of emotional healing around me...
A circle of emotional healing around me...
I place myself within a circle of emotional healing...
Myself, within emotional healing...
I am within emotional healing..."

There is no right or wrong in doing this. Do it in your own way, using your own creativity, inner guidance, and intuition. You may use your own wording, affirm it in your own way. Just have a clear intention: in this case, Emotional Healing.

Repeat and draw the circle over and over with this color, repeating the thoughts, making adjustments, and enhancing them, making the color of the circle more intense, vivid, and uniform. Each time, re-affirm your intention for emotional healing.

Then, pause for a while and look at the circle and think once more what it stands for, what it means. Do you feel the energy? Relax and notice. You can also take some slow, full, deep breaths.

You can enhance and empower this energy even more!

Using the same blue color, design a second larger circle around the first one. Think of what this second larger circle means:

"Greater emotional healing around me...
Myself, within greater emotional healing...
I am in greater emotional healing...
More emotional healing...
Even more emotional healing...
Much more emotional healing...
Around myself and me in the center of it..."

Keep moving the marker around, making the circle bolder and stronger. Do it in a steady, slow, and meditative manner. Keep the above statement in your mind or repeat it out loud. Once more, you can use your own words but focus on your intention for even greater emotional healing.

Make another pause and observe the drawing, and notice how you feel its energy. It works, it starts to manifest! It is manifesting its effects and it is powerful! You can also take some more deep, slow, full breaths.

Now let's take this to the maximum, to its greatest height and power.

Make a third, even larger circle, around the second one. Again, in the color blue. It symbolizes the highest possible level of energy, the greatest possible emotional healing! Absolute, perfect, total, divine emotional healing! Emotional healing on all levels!

Think about this meaning, as you draw the circle, slowly and meditatively. Repeat the circle a few times, over and over, and each time, think or say out loud the following:

"Perfect emotional healing around me...
Myself, in perfect emotional healing...
I am within perfect emotional healing...
The highest level of emotional healing!
The greatest, the supreme emotional healing!
Absolute and perfect emotional healing!
Total and complete emotional healing!
Emotional healing on all levels!"

As always, you can use your own wording, keeping in mind your intention for the highest level of this energy, the greatest possible emotional healing.

Stop and relax once more, noticing and observing everything. Feel the amazing energy and power! Stay for a few moments in this high positive state, receiving and experiencing all that goodness! You can also take some more deep, slow, full breaths.

For this third circle, the third level of this work, you can also use a different color, a golden one. The color gold symbolizes the golden light, the highest spiritual light. The highest level of energy and the highest level of consciousness; super-consciousness, spiritual or divine consciousness. The golden light is the light of Spirit, the Logos, and the Source/the Absolute. It is pure wisdom, pure love, and pure power... infinite wisdom – infinite love – infinite power and perfect wisdom – perfect love – perfect power!

This technique can be done using other colors too. Instead of the blue color, you may use any color you want. You could also make more circles, as many as you want. You control and define what it is that you do, what energy/quality you create, and in what way. Just be aware, know what it is that you're doing, why you are doing each move, the purpose behind each thing.

For example, you can use all the colors, symbolizing different aspects and qualities of emotional healing, or meaning emotional healing on different levels and for different areas of your life.

Try both: emotional healing with a variety of different colors and emotional healing using only the blue color, or with a combination of blue and gold at the end.

You can do just one circle. Leave the drawing as it is and then, after some time has passed or even days later, add a second circle or a third one. Once again, there is no right or wrong; you will be guided. Maybe you make many circles, then decide they are not needed, and so you do the process again, with just one circle this time. Follow your intuition.

Make the process esoterically, calmly, meditatively, and make pauses to feel the energy. Take deep breaths at the beginning and at the end of this exercise and during its practice. Focus on your purpose, clarify your intention, before you begin to design and as you design. Hold your intention. Every now and then, think of why you do what you do, what it means, what it stands for. And at the end, remain in this state, meditating for a few minutes, feeling the wonderful energy, the higher level you have entered!

STRENGTHENING THE PROCESS

There are two ways to reinforce this technique: to fill the circle with color and to add visualization.

COLOR FILLING

Fill the circle with the color blue. Color inside the circle line, slowly and calmly, filling in the white area, and covering your name. You do this so as to fill the space with energy. Your aura and your body. It's like filling your body with color, with energy, with the quality you want – in this case, Emotional Healing!

Think about what you are doing. Have a clear intention in your mind as you fill the circle with color:

"I fill myself with emotional healing, with the energy of emotional healing.
My aura, my energy, my body, is filled with emotional healing, with the energy of emotional healing!
Emotional healing everywhere around me and everywhere inside me...
Emotional healing everywhere around me and everywhere inside me...
Emotional healing everywhere around me and everywhere inside me... "

Or you can use your own words.

Color and fill the whole circle.

You can also fill the space between the first and second circle and between the second and third circle as well, although this is not so important. Do it though, if you feel like it.

Since you have covered your name with color and you can no longer see it, rewrite it down below, below the circles, at the bottom of the paper.

VISUALIZATION

If you want to see more immediate results, add visualization into the process. You can do it at the beginning or at the end.

Or twice, both at the beginning and at the end. This empowers the process to the highest degree!

Gently close your eyes, take some slow and deep breaths, and then let go. Relax your body and mind.

Visualize the circle of emotional healing around you. You can envision a blue, white, or golden circle. Or of some other color. You can also visualize a sphere – this is even better! A blue sphere of emotional healing around you. Or a golden sphere of emotional healing around you. The golden sphere is the highest energy – it is all-inclusive! It is the most intelligent and wise and the strongest and most powerful energy. It is like the sun.

Feel that the sphere is full of energy, light, and power. Full of emotional healing. And you are inside it! You can see or feel this energy as blue energy or as white or golden. In all cases, white or golden energy is ideal. White is the energy of life and it includes everything, all possibilities, while golden is the energy of Spirit and consciousness, of the Supreme Source and it symbolizes the infinite and perfect wisdom, love, and power of the absolute.

You are in the sphere of emotional healing, within the energy of emotional healing!

Mentally, state (or use your own words):

"I am in the sphere of emotional healing, within the energy of emotional healing.

The energy of emotional healing surrounds me; it is all around me.
And the energy of emotional healing is inside me, it is everywhere inside me.
Supreme emotional healing!
Perfect emotional healing!
Absolute emotional healing!
Emotional healing on all levels!"

You do not have to make a second or third circle or a second or third sphere. For the visualization, one circle or one sphere is enough. If, nonetheless, you feel guided to visualize more circles or spheres, go on and do it.

Finally, give thanks from your heart with the utmost love, joy, and gratitude! Open your eyes.

The highest, the most perfect emotional healing, with infinite love and unlimited joy!

GUIDANCE, ANSWERS, CHOICES

Use the following technique to receive inner/higher guidance, to receive answers and support in order to make the best possible choices.

Take some sheets of white paper and a purple marker.

Sit comfortably and relax.

Take a few deep breaths, at a calm and slow pace. Inhale from the nose, slowly and deeply, taking your breath deep down into your belly and lower abdomen. Breathe out from the mouth, blowing the air gently, steadily, and slowly. Do these full, conscious, energetic breaths. They will release any tension, pressure, and burden and will fill you with energy, liveliness, and positivity.

Then, simply relax, and calm down your mind and body totally. Let go, let go completely.

Feel joy and have a wonderful sense of joyful anticipation, thinking about what you are going to do! You are going to give guidance to yourself, you are going to place your personal energy within greater guidance – spiritual and energetic guidance! You are about to bring forth and experience perfect guidance, total guidance, guidance on all levels!

Take the marker and one sheet of paper and write your name in the center of the paper. Your forename and then your surname under it. You can write your official, complete name or the one you use in your daily encounters. You can also use your middle name, if you have one. Simply write it under your forename and above your surname.

You can also just write the initials of your forename and surname. You can even not write down your name at all. Instead, you may write or draw something on the paper that represents/symbolizes you. For instance, you can make a dot, draw a star, or a human stick figure, as a symbol for yourself. What you have in mind – your intention – is the primary and most important element in this work and the design is secondary; it is merely symbolic.

Think that, while using the marker and drawing a circle around your name, this circle symbolizes the energy and the quality you want to bring forth and experience. The ideal state/condition you want to experience. In this case, it is Guidance.

Draw the circle around your complete name. Do it slowly, meditatively. It does not matter how large the circle is – as long as it encircles your name, that is, until it includes you. It does not have to be a perfect circle; it can be clumsy. Also, it does not matter whether you draw the circle in a left or right direction.

Do it slowly and think that what you do has great power, great power in energetic and spiritual terms.

Keep your intention in mind while you draw the circle. What does it mean? Why are you doing this?

Affirm it, either mentally or out loud:

"I create a circle of guidance around me...
A circle of guidance, around me...
I place myself within a circle of guidance...
Myself, within guidance...
I am within guidance..."

You can also repeat the quality/energy:

"Guidance... Guidance... Guidance..."

Or you can repeat both affirmations:

"Guidance... Guidance... Guidance...
I create a circle of guidance around me...
A circle of guidance around me...
I place myself within a circle of guidance...
Myself, within guidance...
I am within guidance..."

There is no right or wrong in doing this. Do it in your own way, using your own creativity, inner guidance, and intuition. You may use your own wording, affirm it in your own way. Just have a clear intention: in this case, Guidance.

Repeat and draw the circle over and over with this color, repeating the thoughts, making adjustments, and enhancing them, making the color of the circle more intense, vivid, and uniform. Each time, re-affirm your intention for guidance.

Then, pause for a while and look at the circle and think once more what it stands for, what it means. Do you feel the energy? Relax and notice. You can also take some slow, full, deep breaths.

You can enhance and empower this energy even more!

Using the same purple color, design a second larger circle around the first one. Think of what this second larger circle means:

"Greater guidance around me...
Myself, within greater guidance...
I am in greater guidance...
More guidance...
Even more guidance...
Much more guidance...
Around myself and me in the center of it..."

Keep moving the marker around, making the circle bolder and stronger. Do it in a steady, slow, and meditative manner. Keep the above statement in your mind or repeat it out loud. Once more, you can use your own words but focus on your intention for even greater guidance.

Make another pause and observe the drawing, and notice how

you feel its energy. It works, it starts to manifest! It is manifesting its effects and it is powerful! You can also take some more deep, slow, full breaths.

Now let's take this to the maximum, to its greatest height and power.

Make a third, even larger circle, around the second one. Again, in the color purple. It symbolizes the highest possible level of energy, the greatest possible guidance! Absolute, perfect, total, divine guidance! Guidance on all levels!

Think about this meaning, as you draw the circle, slowly and meditatively. Repeat the circle a few times, over and over, and each time, think or say out loud the following:

"Perfect guidance around me...
Myself, in perfect guidance...
I am within perfect guidance...
The highest level of guidance!
The greatest, the supreme guidance!
Absolute and perfect guidance!
Total and complete guidance!
Guidance on all levels!"

As always, you can use your own wording, keeping in mind your intention for the highest level of this energy, the greatest possible guidance.

Stop and relax once more, noticing and observing everything.

Feel the amazing energy and power! Stay for a few moments in this high positive state, receiving and experiencing all that goodness! You can also take some more deep, slow, full breaths.

For this third circle, the third level of this work, you can also use a different color, a golden one. The color gold symbolizes the golden light, the highest spiritual light. The highest level of energy and the highest level of consciousness; super-consciousness, spiritual or divine consciousness. The golden light is the light of Spirit, the Logos, and the Source/the Absolute. It is pure wisdom, pure love, and pure power... infinite wisdom – infinite love – infinite power and perfect wisdom – perfect love – perfect power!

This technique can be done using other colors too. Instead of the purple color, you may use any color you want. You could also make more circles, as many as you want. You control and define what it is that you do, what energy/quality you create, and in what way. Just be aware, know what it is that you're doing, why you are doing each move, the purpose behind each thing.

For example, you can use all the colors, symbolizing different aspects and qualities of guidance, or meaning guidance on different levels and for different areas of your life.

Try both: guidance with a variety of different colors and guidance using only the purple color, or with a combination of purple and gold at the end.

You can do just one circle. Leave the drawing as it is and then, after some time has passed or even days later, add a second circle or a third one. Once again, there is no right or wrong; you will be guided. Maybe you make many circles, then decide they are not needed, and so you do the process again, with just one circle this time. Follow your intuition.

Make the process esoterically, calmly, meditatively, and make pauses to feel the energy. Take deep breaths at the beginning and at the end of this exercise and during its practice. Focus on your purpose, clarify your intention, before you begin to design and as you design. Hold your intention. Every now and then, think of why you do what you do, what it means, what it stands for. And at the end, remain in this state, meditating for a few minutes, feeling the wonderful energy, the higher level you have entered!

STRENGTHENING THE PROCESS

There are two ways to reinforce this technique: to fill the circle with color and to add visualization.

COLOR FILLING

Fill the circle with the color purple. Color inside the circle line, slowly and calmly, filling in the white area, and covering your name. You do this so as to fill the space with energy. Your aura and your body. It's like filling your body with color, with energy, with the quality you want – in this case, Guidance!

Think about what you are doing. Have a clear intention in your mind as you fill the circle with color:

"I fill myself with guidance, with the energy of guidance.
My aura, my energy, my body, is filled with guidance, with the energy of guidance!
Guidance everywhere around me and everywhere inside me...
Guidance everywhere around me and everywhere inside me...
Guidance everywhere around me and everywhere inside me..."

Or you can use your own words.

Color and fill the whole circle.

You can also fill the space between the first and second circle and between the second and third circle as well, although this is not so important. Do it though, if you feel like it.

Since you have covered your name with color and you can no longer see it, rewrite it down below, below the circles, at the bottom of the paper.

VISUALIZATION

If you want to see more immediate results, add visualization into the process. You can do it at the beginning or at the end. Or twice, both at the beginning and at the end. This empowers the process to the highest degree!

Gently close your eyes, take some slow and deep breaths, and then let go. Relax your body and mind.

Visualize the circle of guidance around you. You can envision a purple, white, or golden circle. Or of some other color. You can also visualize a sphere – this is even better! A purple sphere of guidance around you. Or a golden sphere of guidance around you. The golden sphere is the highest energy – it is all-inclusive! It is the most intelligent and wise and the strongest and most powerful energy. It is like the sun.

Feel that the sphere is full of energy, light, and power. Full of guidance. And you are inside it! You can see or feel this energy as purple energy or as white or golden. In all cases, white or golden energy is ideal. White is the energy of life and it includes everything, all possibilities, while golden is the energy of Spirit and consciousness, of the Supreme Source and it symbolizes the infinite and perfect wisdom, love, and power of the absolute.

You are in the sphere of guidance, within the energy of guidance!

Mentally, state (or use your own words):

"I am in the sphere of guidance, within the energy of guidance.
The energy of guidance surrounds me; it is all around me.
And the energy of guidance is inside me, it is everywhere inside me.
Supreme guidance!
Perfect guidance!
Absolute guidance!
Guidance on all levels!"

You do not have to make a second or third circle or a second or third sphere. For the visualization, one circle or one sphere is enough. If, nonetheless, you feel guided to visualize more circles or spheres, go on and do it.

Finally, give thanks from your heart with the utmost love, joy, and gratitude! Open your eyes.

The highest, the most perfect guidance, with infinite love and unlimited joy!

WISDOM

For this technique, instead of "wisdom", you can also use the words "illumination" or "enlightenment"; or use all three of them.

Take some sheets of white paper and a violet marker.

Sit comfortably and relax.

Take a few deep breaths, at a calm and slow pace. Inhale from the nose, slowly and deeply, taking your breath deep down into your belly and lower abdomen. Breathe out from the mouth, blowing the air gently, steadily, and slowly. Do these full, conscious, energetic breaths. They will release any tension, pressure, and burden and will fill you with energy, liveliness, and positivity.

Then, simply relax, and calm down your mind and body totally. Let go, let go completely.

Feel joy and have a wonderful sense of joyful anticipation, thinking about what you are going to do! You are going to receive wisdom, you are going to place your personal energy within greater wisdom – spiritual and energetic wisdom! You are about to bring forth and experience perfect wisdom, total wisdom, wisdom on all levels!

Take the marker and one sheet of paper and write your name in the center of the paper. Your forename and then your surname under it. You can write your official, complete name or the one you use in your daily encounters. You can also use your middle name, if you have one. Simply write it under your forename and above your surname.

You can also just write the initials of your forename and surname. You can even not write down your name at all. Instead, you may write or draw something on the paper that represents/symbolizes you. For instance, you can make a dot, draw a star, or a human stick figure, as a symbol for yourself. What you have in mind – your intention – is the primary and most important element in this work and the design is secondary; it is merely symbolic.

Think that, while using the marker and drawing a circle around your name, this circle symbolizes the energy and the quality you want to bring forth and experience. The ideal state/condition you want to experience. In this case, it is Wisdom.

Draw the circle around your complete name. Do it slowly, meditatively. It does not matter how large the circle is – as long as it encircles your name, that is, until it includes you. It does not have to be a perfect circle; it can be clumsy. Also, it does not matter whether you draw the circle in a left or right direction.

Do it slowly and think that what you do has great power, great power in energetic and spiritual terms.

Keep your intention in mind while you draw the circle. What does it mean? Why are you doing this?

Affirm it, either mentally or out loud:

"I create a circle of wisdom around me...
A circle of wisdom, around me...
I place myself within a circle of wisdom...
Myself, within wisdom...
I am within wisdom..."

You can also repeat the quality/energy:

"Wisdom... Wisdom... Wisdom..."

Or you can repeat both affirmations:

"Wisdom... Wisdom... Wisdom...
I create a circle of wisdom around me...
A circle of wisdom around me...
I place myself within a circle of wisdom...
Myself, within wisdom...
I am within wisdom..."

There is no right or wrong in doing this. Do it in your own way, using your own creativity, inner guidance, and intuition. You may use your own wording, affirm it in your own way. Just have a clear intention: in this case, Wisdom.

Repeat and draw the circle over and over with this color, repeating the thoughts, making adjustments, and enhancing them, making the color of the circle more intense, vivid, and uniform. Each time, re-affirm your intention for wisdom.

Then, pause for a while and look at the circle and think once more what it stands for, what it means. Do you feel the energy? Relax and notice. You can also take some slow, full, deep breaths.

You can enhance and empower this energy even more!

Using the same violet color, design a second larger circle around the first one. Think of what this second larger circle means:

"Greater wisdom around me...
Myself, within greater wisdom...
I am in greater wisdom...
More wisdom...
Even more wisdom...
Much more wisdom...
Around myself and me in the center of it..."

Keep moving the marker around, making the circle bolder and stronger. Do it in a steady, slow, and meditative manner. Keep the above statement in your mind or repeat it out loud. Once more, you can use your own words but focus on your intention for even greater wisdom.

Make another pause and observe the drawing, and notice how

you feel its energy. It works, it starts to manifest! It is manifesting its effects and it is powerful! You can also take some more deep, slow, full breaths.

Now let's take this to the maximum, to its greatest height and power.

Make a third, even larger circle, around the second one. Again, in the color violet. It symbolizes the highest possible level of energy, the greatest possible wisdom! Absolute, perfect, total, divine wisdom! Wisdom on all levels!

Think about this meaning, as you draw the circle, slowly and meditatively. Repeat the circle a few times, over and over, and each time, think or say out loud the following:

"Perfect wisdom around me...
Myself, in perfect wisdom...
I am within perfect wisdom...
The highest level of wisdom!
The greatest, the supreme wisdom!
Absolute and perfect wisdom!
Total and complete wisdom!
Wisdom on all levels!"

As always, you can use your own wording, keeping in mind your intention for the highest level of this energy, the greatest possible wisdom.

Stop and relax once more, noticing and observing everything.

Feel the amazing energy and power! Stay for a few moments in this high positive state, receiving and experiencing all that goodness! You can also take some more deep, slow, full breaths.

For this third circle, the third level of this work, you can also use a different color, a golden one. The color gold symbolizes the golden light, the highest spiritual light. The highest level of energy and the highest level of consciousness; super-consciousness, spiritual or divine consciousness. The golden light is the light of Spirit, the Logos, and the Source/the Absolute. It is pure wisdom, pure love, and pure power... infinite wisdom – infinite love – infinite power and perfect wisdom – perfect love – perfect power!

This technique can be done using other colors too. Instead of the violet color, you may use any color you want. You could also make more circles, as many as you want. You control and define what it is that you do, what energy/quality you create, and in what way. Just be aware, know what it is that you're doing, why you are doing each move, the purpose behind each thing.

For example, you can use all the colors, symbolizing different aspects and qualities of wisdom, or meaning wisdom on different levels and for different areas of your life.

Try both: wisdom with a variety of different colors and wisdom using only the violet color, or with a combination of violet and gold at the end.

You can do just one circle. Leave the drawing as it is and then, after some time has passed or even days later, add a second circle or a third one. Once again, there is no right or wrong; you will be guided. Maybe you make many circles, then decide they are not needed, and so you do the process again, with just one circle this time. Follow your intuition.

Make the process esoterically, calmly, meditatively, and make pauses to feel the energy. Take deep breaths at the beginning and at the end of this exercise and during its practice. Focus on your purpose, clarify your intention, before you begin to design and as you design. Hold your intention. Every now and then, think of why you do what you do, what it means, what it stands for. And at the end, remain in this state, meditating for a few minutes, feeling the wonderful energy, the higher level you have entered!

STRENGTHENING THE PROCESS

There are two ways to reinforce this technique: to fill the circle with color and to add visualization.

COLOR FILLING

Fill the circle with the color violet. Color inside the circle line, slowly and calmly, filling in the white area, and covering your name. You do this so as to fill the space with energy. Your aura and your body. It's like filling your body with color, with energy, with the quality you want – in this case, Wisdom!

Think about what you are doing. Have a clear intention in your mind as you fill the circle with color:

"I fill myself with wisdom, with the energy of wisdom.
My aura, my energy, my body, is filled with wisdom, with the energy of wisdom!
Wisdom everywhere around me and everywhere inside me...
Wisdom everywhere around me and everywhere inside me...
Wisdom everywhere around me and everywhere inside me... "

Or you can use your own words.

Color and fill the whole circle.

You can also fill the space between the first and second circle and between the second and third circle as well, although this is not so important. Do it though, if you feel like it.

Since you have covered your name with color and you can no longer see it, rewrite it down below, below the circles, at the bottom of the paper.

VISUALIZATION

If you want to see more immediate results, add visualization into the process. You can do it at the beginning or at the end. Or twice, both at the beginning and at the end. This empowers the process to the highest degree!

Gently close your eyes, take some slow and deep breaths, and then let go. Relax your body and mind.

Visualize the circle of wisdom around you. You can envision a violet, white, or golden circle. Or of some other color. You can also visualize a sphere – this is even better! A violet sphere of wisdom around you. Or a golden sphere of wisdom around you. The golden sphere is the highest energy – it is all-inclusive! It is the most intelligent and wise and the strongest and most powerful energy. It is like the sun.

Feel that the sphere is full of energy, light, and power. Full of wisdom. And you are inside it! You can see or feel this energy as violet energy or as white or golden. In all cases, white or golden energy is ideal. White is the energy of life and it includes everything, all possibilities, while golden is the energy of Spirit and consciousness, of the Supreme Source and it symbolizes the infinite and perfect wisdom, love, and power of the absolute.

You are in the sphere of wisdom, within the energy of wisdom!

Mentally, state (or use your own words):

"I am in the sphere of wisdom, within the energy of wisdom.
The energy of wisdom surrounds me; it is all around me.
And the energy of wisdom is inside me, it is everywhere inside me.
Supreme wisdom!
Perfect wisdom!
Absolute wisdom!
Wisdom on all levels!"

You do not have to make a second or third circle or a second or third sphere. For the visualization, one circle or one sphere is enough. If, nonetheless, you feel guided to visualize more circles or spheres, go on and do it.

Finally, give thanks from your heart with the utmost love, joy, and gratitude! Open your eyes.

The highest, the most perfect wisdom, with infinite love and unlimited joy!

Also by Georgios Mylonas (Geom!*)

Healing, Spiritual, and Esoteric Meditations
Angelic Invocations
Angelic Symbols
Angelic Mysticism & Meditations
The Golden Codes of Shamballa
How to Cleanse the Energy of Your Space
Higher Abundance
Higher Love
Higher Healing

Made in the USA
Monee, IL
12 January 2024